Contents

About *Daily Geography Practice*

Daily Geography Practice is based on the eighteen National Geography Standards and is designed to support any geography and social studies curriculums that you may be using in your classroom.

36 Weekly Sections

Teacher Page

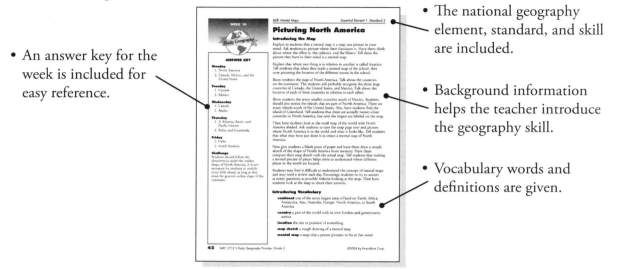

- An answer key for the week is included for easy reference.

- The national geography element, standard, and skill are included.

- Background information helps the teacher introduce the geography skill.

- Vocabulary words and definitions are given.

Please note that the skills in this book should be taught in direct instruction, and not used as independent practice. Teachers are encouraged to use other reference maps and globes to aid in instruction. Most of the questions can be answered by studying the map or globe. There are some questions, however, that specifically relate to the lesson given by the teacher at the beginning of the week. Review daily the information presented in "Introducing the Map."

Map Page

A map or globe illustrates the geography skills emphasized during the week. Use the overhead transparency of the map or globe provided at the back of the book to aid in whole-class instruction. Reproduce the map or globe for each student to use as a reference for the questions.

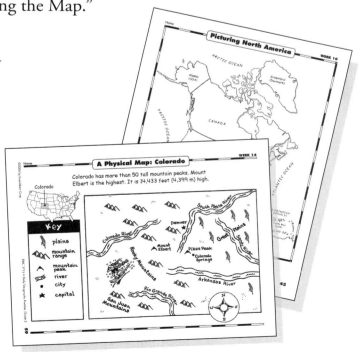

Question Pages

There are two geography questions for each day of the week. The questions progress in difficulty from Monday to Friday. The challenge question at the end of the week asks students to add a feature to the map. Outside references are often required to answer the challenge question.

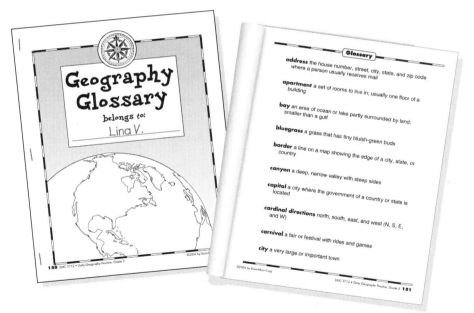

Picturing North America — WEEK 10

Thursday
1. How many oceans border North America? Name them.

2. Name the two countries that border southern Mexico.

Friday
1. Name the largest island country east of Mexico.

2. Name the continent that is south of North America.

Challenge
On the map, trace the outline shape of North America in Place a blank piece of paper over the map. Trace over that show through onto the blank piece of paper. Look drawing of North America. Close your eyes and make picture of the shape of North America.

Picturing North America — WEEK 10

Monday
1. Which continent is shown on the map?

2. Name the three largest countries on the continent.

Tuesday
1. Which large country is north of the United States?

2. Which large country is south of the United States?

Wednesday
1. Which large country has lots of islands to the north?

2. Which U.S. state borders Canada and not the U.S.?

Additional Resources

Geography Glossary

Reproduce the glossary pages and cover for students to use as an easy reference booklet throughout the year.

Map Transparencies

Also included are 36 black-and-white transparencies of the maps and globes in the book. Use overhead pens to highlight or mark special features as you discuss the week's lesson and the accompanying questions.

The National Geography Standards

The National Geography Standards includes six essential elements that highlight the major components of geography. Under the six major categories are the eighteen standards that focus on general areas in geography that children are expected to know and understand.

Essential Element 1: The World in Spatial Terms

Geography studies the relationships between people, places, and environments by mapping information about them into a spatial context. The geographically informed person knows and understands the following:

Standard 1 . . . . **Weeks 1–8**
how to use maps and other geographic representations, tools, and technologies to acquire, process, and report information from a spatial perspective,

Standard 2 . . . . **Weeks 9–10**
how to use mental maps to organize information about people, places, and environments in a spatial context, and

Standard 3 . . . . **Weeks 11–12**
how to analyze the spatial organization of people, places, and environments on Earth's surface.

Essential Element 2: Places and Regions

The identities and lives of individuals and peoples are rooted in particular places and in those human constructs called regions. The geographically informed person knows and understands the following:

Standard 4 . . . . **Weeks 13–18**
the physical and human characteristics of places,

Standard 5 . . . . **Weeks 19–22**
that people create regions to interpret Earth's complexity, and

Standard 6 . . . . **Weeks 23–24**
how culture and experience influence people's perceptions of places and regions.

Essential Element 3: Physical Systems

Physical processes shape Earth's surface and interact with plant and animal life to create, sustain, and modify the ecosystems. The geographically informed person knows and understands the following:

Standard 7 . . . . **Week 25**
the physical processes that shape the patterns of Earth's surface, and

Standard 8 . . . . **Week 26**
the characteristics and spatial distribution of ecosystems on Earth's surface.

Essential Element 4: Human Systems

People are central to geography in that human activities help shape Earth's surface, human settlements and structures are part of Earth's surface, and humans compete for control of Earth's surface. The geographically informed person knows and understands the following:

Essential Element 5: Environment and Society

The physical environment is modified by human activities, largely as a consequence of the ways in which human societies value and use Earth's natural resources. Human activities are also influenced by Earth's physical features and processes. The geographically informed person knows and understands the following:

Essential Element 6: The Uses of Geography

Knowledge of geography enables people to develop an understanding of the relationships between people, places, and environments over time—that is, of Earth as it was, is, and might be. The geographically informed person knows and understands the following:

Daily Geography

ANSWER KEY

Monday
1. Earth
2. ball

Tuesday
1. the equator
2. Any two of the following:
   North America, South America,
   Antarctica, Australia, Europe,
   Africa, Asia

Wednesday
1. the North Pole
2. the South Pole

Thursday
1. south
2. south

Friday
1. Answers will vary.
2. Answers will vary.

Challenge
On all three globes, students should
color the oceans blue and the
continents green.

What Is a Globe?

Introducing the Globes

Show students the classroom globe. Explain to them that the Earth is very large. People can only see part of it at a time. Tell students that a globe is a small model used to show the whole Earth. Like Earth, a globe is shaped like a ball. The globe shows Earth's largest land areas, called continents. The largest water areas are called oceans. The globe also shows an imaginary line called the equator that runs around the center of Earth.

Show students the pictures of the globes. Talk about the top globe picture and how it shows the shape of a globe. Explain that a picture of a globe can only show one half of the round Earth at a time. Have students look at the two other pictures of globes that show two views of Earth. Point out the equator and show how it goes around the surface of the Earth. Show students the North Pole and the South Pole. Also name the continents and the oceans shown on each globe picture.

Be sure to read the caption with students and review the vocabulary for the week.

Introducing Vocabulary

continent one of the seven largest areas of land on Earth: Africa, Antarctica, Asia, Australia, Europe, North America, or South America

equator an imaginary line that runs around the surface of the Earth

globe a round model of the Earth

North Pole the most northern point on Earth

ocean a large body of salt water

South Pole the most southern point on Earth

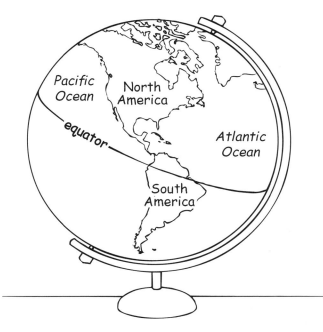

A globe is a model of Earth. It is shaped like a ball.

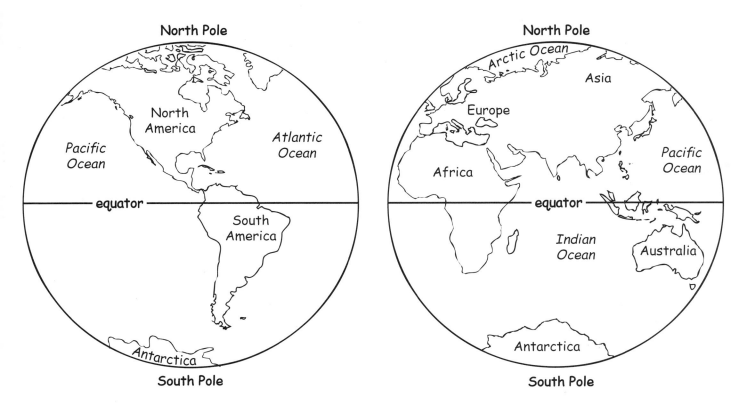

A globe shows an imaginary line called the equator.
The equator runs around the center of the Earth.

What Is a Globe?

Monday

1. A globe is a model of _____ .

2. A globe and Earth are shaped like a _____ .

Tuesday

1. Name the imaginary line shown on the globes.

   _____

2. Name two continents.

   _____

   _____

Wednesday

1. What is the most northern point on Earth called?

   _____

2. What is the most southern point on Earth called?

   _____

What Is a Globe?

Thursday

1. Is Australia south or north of the equator?

   _____

2. Is most of South America north or south of the equator?

   _____

Friday

1. In which continent do you live?

   _____

2. Do you live north or south of the equator?

   _____

Challenge

On all three globes, color the oceans blue.
Color the continents green.

Daily Geography

What Is a Map?

Introducing the Map

Explain to students that a map is a drawing of a place as if seen from above. The main purpose of a map is to show where things or places are located. A map is different from a globe because a map is a flat picture and a globe is round like a ball. A map can show a close-up view of an area, and it is easy to carry around or print in a book. Also, a map can show us how far one place is from another. Explain that maps can show different types of places and things, for example: a world map, a state map, a city map, and a neighborhood map.

Show students the map of the world. Explain that the surface of the Earth is made up of large landmasses, called continents, and large bodies of water, called oceans. Explain that maps show the continents and oceans by depicting lines, called borders. The borders on the world map show the outside edges of the continents and oceans. This map shows the seven continents and four oceans.

Be sure to read the caption with students and review the vocabulary words that are included for the week.

Introducing Vocabulary

border a line on a map showing the edge of a city, state, or country

continent one of the seven largest areas of land on Earth: Africa, Antarctica, Asia, Australia, Europe, North America, or South America

map a drawing showing features of an area

ocean a large body of salt water

ANSWER KEY

Monday

1. a drawing showing features of an area
2. the world

Tuesday

1. seven
2. Any three of the following: Africa, Antarctica, Asia, Australia, North America, South America, or Europe

Wednesday

1. four
2. Pacific Ocean, Arctic Ocean, Indian Ocean, Atlantic Ocean

Thursday

1. South America, North America, Africa, Europe
2. Australia and Antarctica

Friday

1. Answers will vary, for example: I live in North America.
2. Answers will vary, for example: My closest neighbor is South America.

Challenge

Students should color:
- the oceans blue
- North America yellow
- South America red
- Antarctica gray
- Africa purple
- Europe orange
- Asia green
- Australia brown

Name

What Is a Map?

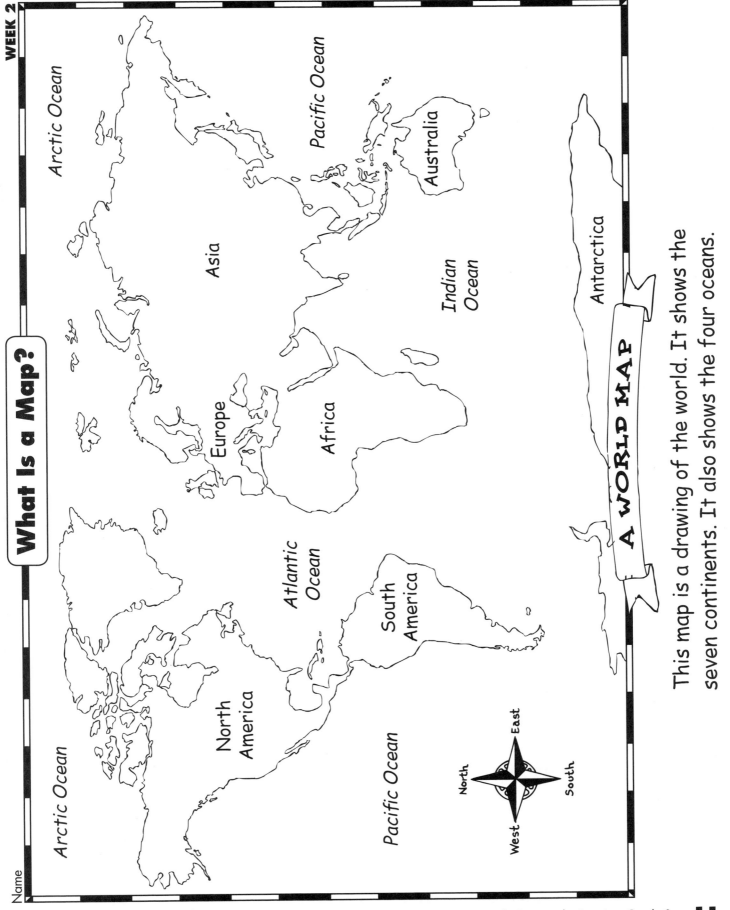

A WORLD MAP

This map is a drawing of the world. It shows the seven continents. It also shows the four oceans.

What Is a Map?

Monday

1. What is a map?

    _____

    _____

2. What does this map show?

    _____

Tuesday

1. How many continents does this map show? _____

2. Write the names of three continents.

    _____

    _____

Wednesday

1. How many oceans are on this map? _____

2. Write the names of the oceans.

    _____

    _____

What Is a Map?

Thursday

1. Which continents border the Atlantic Ocean?

   _____

   _____

2. Which two continents do <u>not</u> touch any other continent?

   _____

Friday

1. On which continent do you live?

   _____

2. Which continent is your closest neighbor?

   _____

Challenge

- Color the oceans blue.
- Color North America yellow.
- Color South America red.
- Color Antarctica gray.

- Color Africa purple.
- Color Europe orange.
- Color Asia green.
- Color Australia brown.

WEEK 3

Parts of a Map

Introducing the Map

Explain to students that in order to understand the information on a map they must look at certain parts of the map. The first part is the title, which tells readers what the map is about. Another common part is the map key. Explain to students that a map key is a list of symbols used to represent objects and places on a map. Explain that the symbols on a map are pictures that stand for something real. Share with students that most maps have a common symbol called a compass rose. Tell students that a compass rose is a symbol that shows the four main directions on a map. The four main directions are North, South, East, and West. These are also called cardinal directions.

Show students the map of Sandy Shores. Study the map and point out each part of the map. As a class, read the caption so students understand which parts are labeled on this map. Then ask students to locate and describe the title. Ask students to locate the map key. As a class, read the definition of a map key. Remind students that each symbol in the map key represents a feature of the map. Have students find the hotel on the key and on the map. Ask students to name the hotel.

Then ask students to locate the compass rose. As a class, read what a compass rose shows. Point out that most compass roses use initials to indicate the cardinal directions. N–North; S–South; E–East; W–West. Have students practice finding places on the map. Ask them to locate the shop on the map. Ask students in which direction the shop is from the lake. The shop is north of the lake.

Review the parts of the map and the vocabulary throughout the week to check for understanding.

Introducing Vocabulary

cardinal directions north, south, east, and west (N, S, E, and W)

compass rose a symbol that shows directions on a map

lake a large body of fresh water surrounded by land

map key a list that explains the symbols on a map

symbol a picture that stands for something real

title the name of a map

ANSWER KEY

Monday
1. Sandy Shores
2. a list that explains the symbols on a map

Tuesday
1. Any three of the following: lake, gas station, restaurant, hotel, or shop
2. restaurant

Wednesday
1. directions on a map
2. north, east, south, west

Thursday
1. 2; First Avenue and Second Avenue
2. east and west

Friday
1. the west end
2. Shop 4 Less and Lupe's Taco Shack

Challenge
Students' choice of title should reflect subject matter on the map.

The parts of the map include a title, a map key, and a compass rose.

This is the title. The title tells the name of the map.

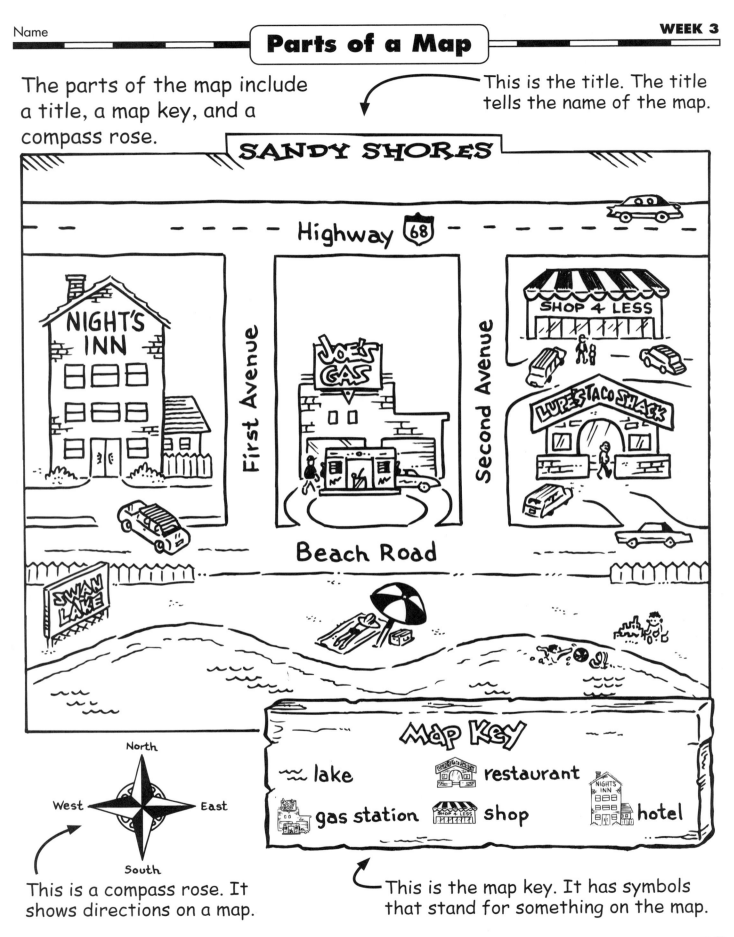

SANDY SHORES

Highway 68

NIGHT'S INN

First Avenue

Second Avenue

JOE'S GAS

SHOP 4 LESS

LUPE'S TACO SHACK

Beach Road

SWAN LAKE

Map Key

~~ lake   restaurant

gas station   shop   hotel

North

West   East

South

This is a compass rose. It shows directions on a map.

This is the map key. It has symbols that stand for something on the map.

Parts of a Map

Monday

1. What is the title of the map?

   _____

2. What is a map key?

   _____

   _____

Tuesday

1. Write the names of three symbols used in the map key.

   _____

2. Name the symbol used for Lupe's Taco Shack.

   _____

Wednesday

1. What does a compass rose show?

   _____

2. Which directions are shown on this compass rose?

   _____

Parts of a Map

Thursday

1. How many avenues are on this map? What are their names?

   _____

2. Does Highway 68 run east and west, or north and south?

   _____

Friday

1. Is Night's Inn on the west or east end of Beach Road?

   _____

2. Which two businesses are east of Second Avenue?

   _____

Challenge

What would you call this small town? Write a new title for this map. Write the new title on the map.

WEEK 4

Daily Geography

Intermediate Directions

Introducing the Map

Tell students that a compass rose is a symbol that shows the directions on a map. The four main directions are north, south, east, and west. These are also called cardinal directions. Tell students that the second type of directions found on a compass rose are called intermediate directions. Explain that intermediate directions are between the main directions on a compass rose. Tell students that there are four intermediate directions, northeast, northwest, southeast, and southwest. Explain that we use intermediate directions when we need to know a more exact direction.

Show students the map of the neighborhood. Have students find the compass rose and put one finger on north and another finger on east. Ask them which direction is between north and east (northeast). Explain that when you name intermediate directions, you combine *north* or *south* with *east* or *west* to make one word. Point out that *north* and *south* always begin the intermediate direction. For example, to say *northeast* is correct. To say *eastnorth* is incorrect. Explain that abbreviations are used for intermediate directions: northeast—NE; northwest—NW; southeast—SE; southwest—SE.

Have students look at the police station. Ask them in which direction the police station is from the library. The police station is north of the library. Then ask students in which direction the post office is from the police station. The post office is southeast of the police station.

You may wish to ask more directional questions to check for understanding. Review vocabulary with the students as needed throughout the week.

Introducing Vocabulary

cardinal directions north, south, east, and west (N, S, E, and W)

compass rose a symbol that shows directions on a map

intermediate directions northeast, northwest, southeast, southwest (NE, NW, SE, SW)

ANSWER KEY

Monday
1. northeast, northwest, southeast, southwest
2. NE, NW, SE, SW

Tuesday
1. the post office
2. the library

Wednesday
1. northwest
2. northeast

Thursday
1. the police station
2. north and south

Friday
1. east
2. a fountain

Challenge

Students should have drawn a book in the southeast corner of the library.

Students should have drawn a flagpole in the southwest corner of the school.

Intermediate Directions

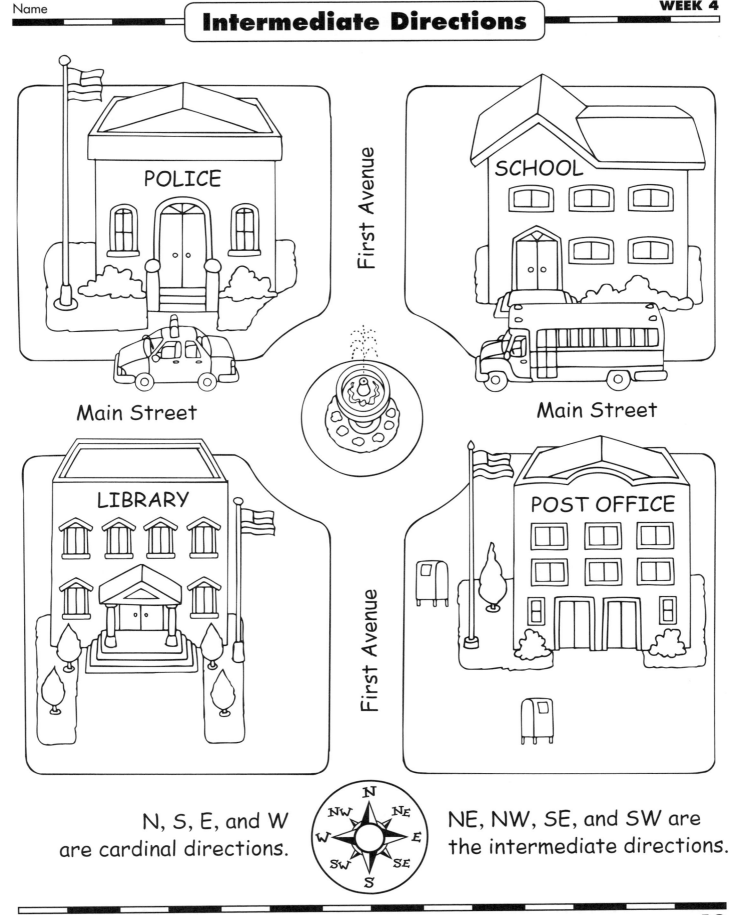

POLICE

First Avenue

SCHOOL

Main Street

Main Street

LIBRARY

First Avenue

POST OFFICE

N, S, E, and W are cardinal directions.

NE, NW, SE, and SW are the intermediate directions.

Intermediate Directions

Monday

1. What are the intermediate directions on the compass rose?

   _____

   _____

2. Write the letters used for the four intermediate directions.

   _____

Tuesday

1. Which building is east of the library?

   _____

2. Which building is southwest of the school?

   _____

Wednesday

1. Start at the post office. In which direction is the police station?

   _____

2. Start at the library. In which direction is the school?

   _____

Intermediate Directions

Thursday

1. Which building is northwest of the post office?

   _____

2. Does First Avenue run east and west or north and south?

   _____

Friday

1. Start at the west end of Main Street. In which direction is the fountain?

   _____

2. What is found where Main Street and First Avenue cross?

   _____

Challenge

On the map, draw a book in the southeast corner of the library.

Draw a flagpole in the southwest corner of the school.

A Map Grid

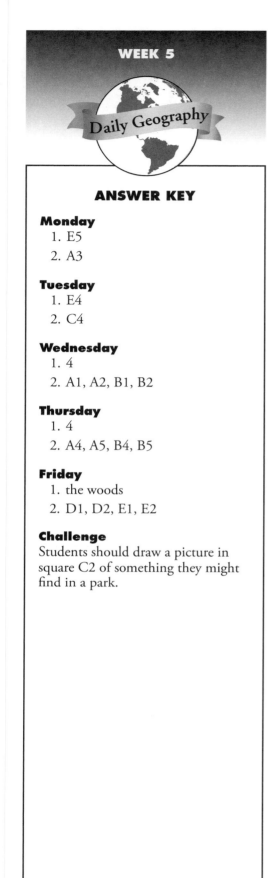

WEEK 5

Daily Geography

ANSWER KEY

Monday
1. E5
2. A3

Tuesday
1. E4
2. C4

Wednesday
1. 4
2. A1, A2, B1, B2

Thursday
1. 4
2. A4, A5, B4, B5

Friday
1. the woods
2. D1, D2, E1, E2

Challenge
Students should draw a picture in square C2 of something they might find in a park.

Introducing the Map

Share with students that some maps have lines on them. These lines form a pattern called a grid. Tell students the definition of a grid. Expand on the definition by telling students that the squares formed by the grid are marked with letters and numbers. On some maps, the letters run across the top and the numbers run down the side. On other maps, they may find the opposite is true—the numbers run across the top and letters run down the side. Explain to students that grids on maps help people locate specific things on a map more readily.

Show students the map of the park. Have students look at the map key. Discuss the symbols in the key and have students find the symbols on the map. Point out the grid lines on the map. Show students how the grid lines form squares. Have students find the letter "A" at the side of the map. Then have the students find the number "1" at the top of the map. The first square in the top row is called A1. Ask students what is located in A1 (picnic table).

Give students other grid locations to check for understanding. Review the concept of a map grid and vocabulary words throughout the week.

Introducing Vocabulary

grid a pattern of lines that form squares

map key a list that explains the symbols on a map

A Map Grid

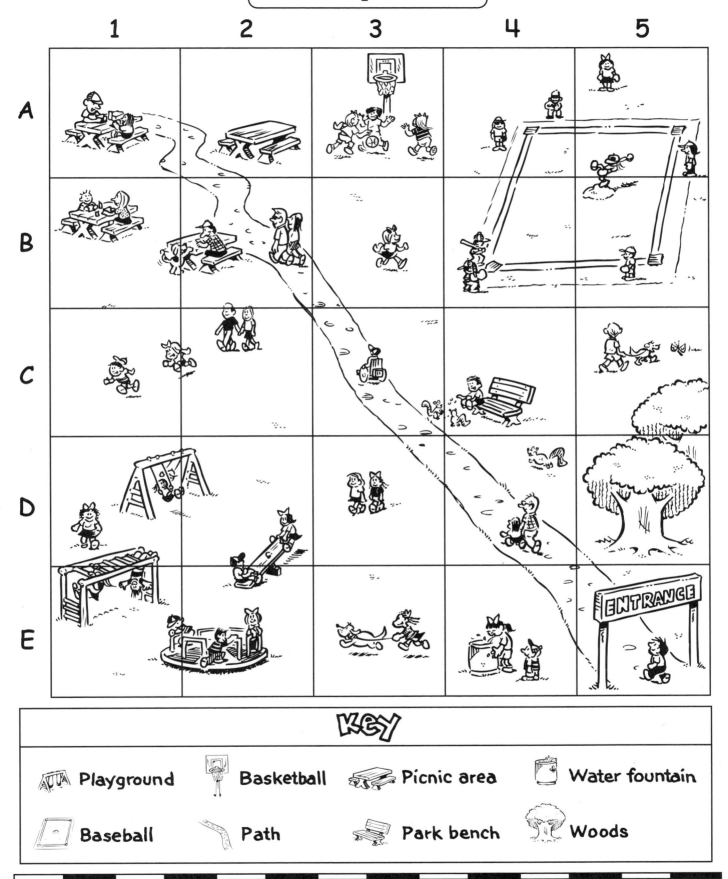

A Map Grid

Monday

1. In which square would you find the park entrance?

_____

2. In which square would you go to play basketball?

_____

Tuesday

1. In which square can you get a drink of water?

_____

2. In which square can you rest on a park bench?

_____

Wednesday

1. How many squares does the picnic area include?

_____

2. Name the squares for the picnic area.

_____

A Map Grid

Thursday

1. How many squares does the baseball diamond include?

    _____

2. Name the squares for the baseball area.

    _____

Friday

1. What is above square E5?

    _____

2. The playground equipment is in which four squares?

    _____

Challenge

Find square C2. Draw a picture in this square of something you might see in a park.

ANSWER KEY

Monday
1. 1, 2, 3, 4, 5
2. A, B, C, D, E, F, G

Tuesday
1. Gadsden
2. Tuscaloosa

Wednesday
1. C3
2. G1

Thursday
1. Decatur
2. A3

Friday
1. Montgomery; D3 and D4
2. A map index lists the cities in Alabama. It also shows the grid squares in which the cities are found.

Challenge
Students should color square E2 red and G4 green.

A Map Grid and a Map Index

Introducing the Map

Tell students that some maps have lines on them that form a pattern called a grid. Review the definition of a grid. Tell students that the squares formed by the grid are marked with letters and numbers. On some maps the letters run across the top and the numbers run down the side. On other maps, they may find the opposite is true—the numbers run across the top and letters run down the side. Remind students that grids on maps help people more readily locate specific things on a map.

Show students the grid map of the state of Alabama. Have students find the letter "C" at the side of the map. Then have the students find the number "2" at the top of the map. The second square in the third row is called C2. Ask students what is located in C2 (Tuscaloosa). You may choose to give students another grid location to check for understanding.

Point out the map index. Explain to students that a map index is included on some maps. Tell students that a map index is like an index in a book. The index at the back of the book leads students to a specific place in the book. A map index leads students to a specific place on a map. Read the names of the cities and their grid locations on the index.

Review the concepts of a map grid and index throughout the week. Also, review vocabulary as needed.

Introducing Vocabulary

capital a city where the government of a country or state is located

city a very large or important town

grid a pattern of lines that form squares

index a list of place names and the grid squares where they are located

state a group of people united under one government; a state can be a whole country or part of a country, such as the United States

Alabama

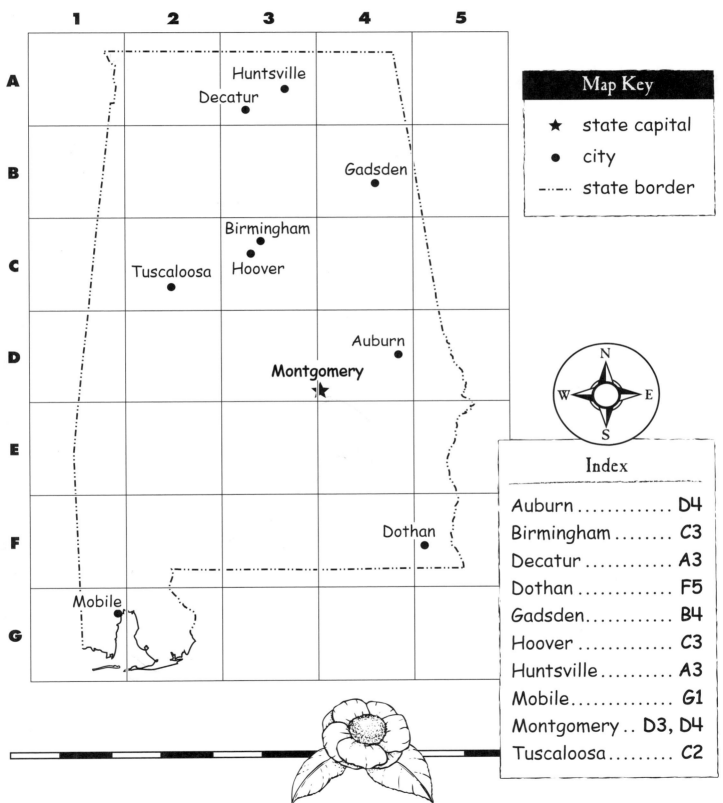

Map Key

★ state capital

● city

-··-··- state border

Index

Auburn............. D4
Birmingham........ C3
Decatur........... A3
Dothan............ F5
Gadsden........... B4
Hoover........... C3
Huntsville......... A3
Mobile............ G1
Montgomery.. D3, D4
Tuscaloosa........ C2

A Map Grid and a Map Index

Monday

1. Which numbers are on this map grid?

   _____

2. Which letters are on the map grid?

   _____

Tuesday

1. Which city is in square B4?

   _____

2. Which city is in square C2?

   _____

Wednesday

1. In which square are the cities of Birmingham and Hoover?

   _____

2. In which square is the city of Mobile?

   _____

A Map Grid and a Map Index

Thursday

1. Huntsville shares a square with which other city?

   _____

2. In which square is Decatur?

   _____

Friday

1. What is the capital of Alabama? In which two squares is it?

   _____

2. What does the map index show?

   _____

   _____

Challenge

On the map:

• Color square E2 red.

• Color square G4 green.

WEEK 7

A Map Key

Introducing the Map

Tell students that a map key is a list of symbols used to represent objects and places on a map. Explain that the symbols on a map are pictures that stand for something real.

Have students look at the map of the state of Illinois. Ask students to locate the map key. Point out that this map key includes seven symbols. A star symbol is used to denote the capital city; a shaded box symbol is used to denote large cities; a large dot is used to denote medium cities; and a small dot is used to denote small towns. A wavy line symbol is used to denote rivers, and an oval symbol is used to denote a lake. Review the definitions of *capital, city, town, river,* and *lake*. A dashed line with dots represents state borders.

Include Illinois' borders in your discussion. Use the small map of the United States to review the borders of Illinois. Point out that Indiana, Kentucky, Missouri, Iowa, Wisconsin, and Lake Michigan share borders with Illinois. Also point out the rivers that border the state, as well.

Introducing Vocabulary

border a line on a map showing the edge of a city, state, or country

capital a city where the government of a country or state is located

city a very large or important town

lake a large body of fresh water surrounded by land

map key a list that explains the symbols on a map

river a large stream that flows into a larger river, lake, sea, or ocean

state a group of people united under one government; a state can be a whole country or part of a country such as the United States

symbol a picture that stands for something real

town an area where people live and work; usually smaller than a city

---

ANSWER KEY

Monday
1. Springfield
2. Chicago

Tuesday
1. Decatur, Rockford, Aurora, Peoria
2. Bentley, Mt. Pleasant

Wednesday
1. Mississippi River and Wabash River
2. Illinois River, Kaskaskia River

Thursday
1. Rockford
2. Lake Michigan

Friday
1. Chicago
2. Indiana

Challenge
Students should write the names of the following border states on the map: Wisconsin, Iowa, Missouri, Kentucky, Indiana.

A Map Key

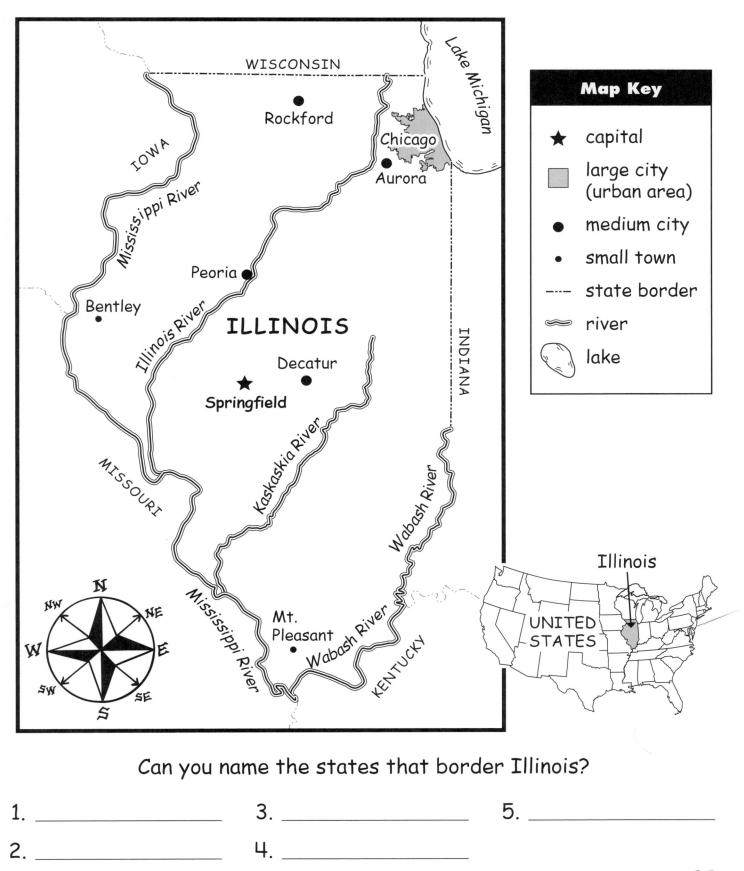

Can you name the states that border Illinois?

1. _____   3. _____   5. _____

2. _____   4. _____

A Map Key

Monday

1. What is the name of the capital city?

   _____

2. What is the name of the large city shown on the map?

   _____

Tuesday

1. Write the name of each medium-size city.

   _____

   _____

2. Write the name of each small town.

   _____

Wednesday

1. Write the names of the two rivers that are borders.

   _____

2. Write the names of the two rivers that are not borders.

   _____

A Map Key

Thursday

1. Write the name of the medium-size city that is close to the Wisconsin border.

   _____

2. Write the name of the lake that shares a border with Illinois.

   _____

Friday

1. Write the name of the large city that shares a border with Lake Michigan.

   _____

2. Write the name of the border state that is east of Decatur and Aurora.

   _____

Challenge

On the map, write the names of the states that border Illinois.

WEEK 8

Daily Geography

ANSWER KEY

Monday
1. 10
2. Austin

Tuesday
1. second
2. northern

Wednesday
1. 50
2. 100

Thursday
1. western
2. Brownsville

Friday
1. 4
2. 400

Challenge
Students should write on the map page that Houston is about 300 miles (3 inches) from Brownsville.

A Map Scale

Introducing the Map

Explain to students that certain elements are found on maps, such as: a title, key, compass rose, and a map grid. Tell students that places and things on a map are shown much smaller than their real size. A map shows things much closer together than they are in real life. Some maps have a map scale on them. Explain that a scale is like a map ruler: it is used to measure distances on a map.

A scale defines the distances between places on a map. A bar scale is used for this lesson. A bar scale uses a graphic to show the relationship between the distance on a map and the actual distance represented.

Show students the map of the state of Texas. Have them look at the scale at the bottom of the map. They will notice that the scale is in both standard and metric measurements. For this lesson, students will use a standard ruler. First, have students use their rulers to measure 100 miles on the scale. The answer is one inch. Therefore, one inch on the map represents 100 miles. Have students use their rulers to find the distance between Austin and San Antonio. The distance is about one inch on the map which represents 100 miles.

Point out that other distances and measurements have been given for reference on the map page. Have students measure the distance from El Paso to Corpus Christi (about 6 inches). Tell them that they will have to add 100 miles for each inch (100 + 100 + 100 + 100 + 100 + 100 = 600). So the actual distance is 600 miles.

Please note that the bar scale and distances have been simplified for this level. Students should estimate measurements to the nearest 1/2 inch. You may choose to introduce this skill at a later time in the year when the students are more familiar with measurement.

Introducing Vocabulary

map scale a graphic that compares the distance on a map to the distance it represents

state a group of people united under one government; a state can be a whole country or part of a country, such as the United States

A Map Scale

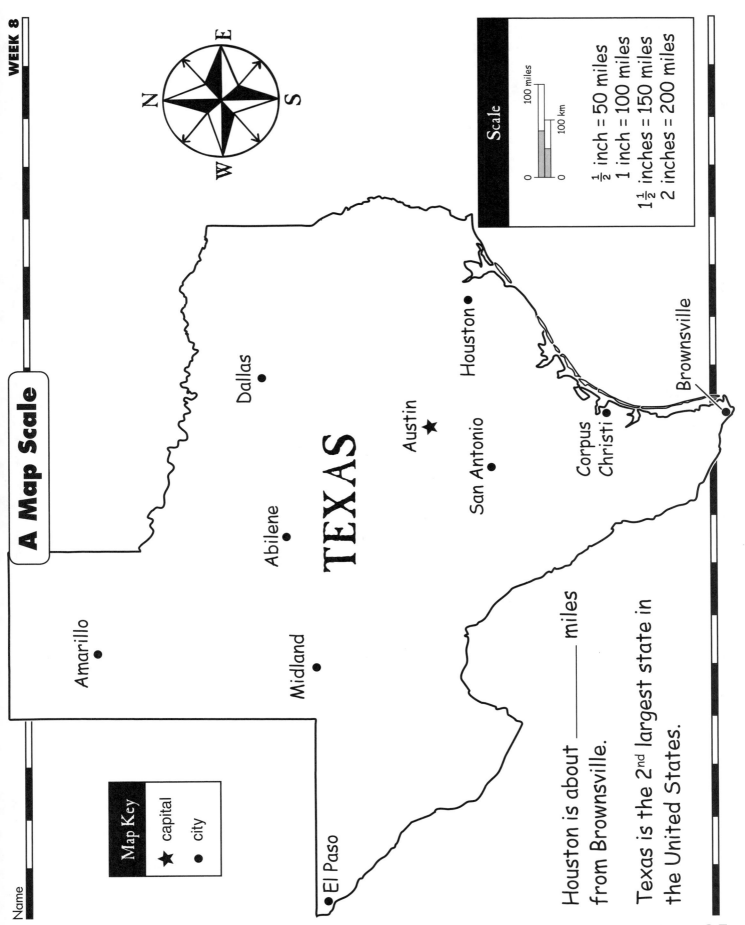

Map Key
★ capital
• city

TEXAS

Amarillo •
• El Paso
Midland •
Abilene •
Dallas •
Austin ★
San Antonio •
Houston •
Corpus Christi •
Brownsville •

N E S W

Scale
100 miles
100 km
0   0

½ inch = 50 miles
1 inch = 100 miles
1½ inches = 150 miles
2 inches = 200 miles

Houston is about _____ miles from Brownsville.

Texas is the 2nd largest state in the United States.

Name

A Map Scale

Monday

1. How many cities are shown on this map?

   _____

2. What is the capital of Texas?

   _____

Tuesday

1. Texas is the _____ largest state in the United States.

2. Is Amarillo in northern or southern Texas?

   _____

Wednesday

1. On the map scale, ½ inch = _____ miles.

2. On the map scale, 1 inch = _____ miles.

A Map Scale

Thursday

1. Is El Paso in eastern or western Texas?

   _____

2. Which city shown on the map is the farthest south?

   _____

Friday

1. On the map, El Paso is about _____ inches from Abilene.

2. About how many miles is El Paso from Abilene?

   _____

Challenge

Measure the distance in inches between Houston and Brownsville. Use the scale to find about how many miles that represents. Write your answer on the map page.

WEEK 9

Daily Geography

Picturing the United States

Introducing the Map

Explain to students that a mental map is a map you picture in your mind.

Ask students to picture the inside of their house. Ask them to think about where the kitchen is, their bedroom, and the bathroom. Tell them the picture they have in their mind is a mental map.

Explain that where one thing is in relation to another is called location. Tell students that when they made a mental map of the inside of their house, they were picturing the location of the rooms in their house.

Have students look at the map of the United States. Talk about the shape of the U.S. Have them trace the outline shape with their fingers. Point out that there are 48 states that are connected. Give students a blank piece of paper to place on top of the U.S. map. Have them trace the outline shape of the U.S.

Show students the small maps of Alaska and Hawaii. Talk about how the states of Alaska and Hawaii are part of the United States, but they are not connected. Point out the small map with the United States shaded. Then, give students a blank piece of paper and have them draw the shape of the United States from memory. Have them compare their map sketch with the actual map. Tell students that making a mental picture of places helps them to understand where places in the world are located.

Students may find it difficult to understand the concept of mental maps and may need a review each day. Encourage students to try to answer as many questions as possible without looking at the map. Then have students look at the map to check their answers.

Introducing Vocabulary

location the site or position of something

map sketch a rough drawing of a mental map

mental map a map that a person pictures in his or her mind

state a group of people united under one government; a state can be a whole country or part of a country, such as the United States

ANSWER KEY

Monday
1. western
2. east

Tuesday
1. Any two of the following: Washington, Oregon, California, Alaska, or Hawaii
2. Atlantic Ocean

Wednesday
1. 5
2. Alaska and Hawaii

Thursday
1. Canada; Arctic and Pacific Oceans
2. south

Friday
1. north
2. south

Challenge
Students should draw a map of the outline shape of the United States. Then look at the real map to see how they did.

Picturing the United States

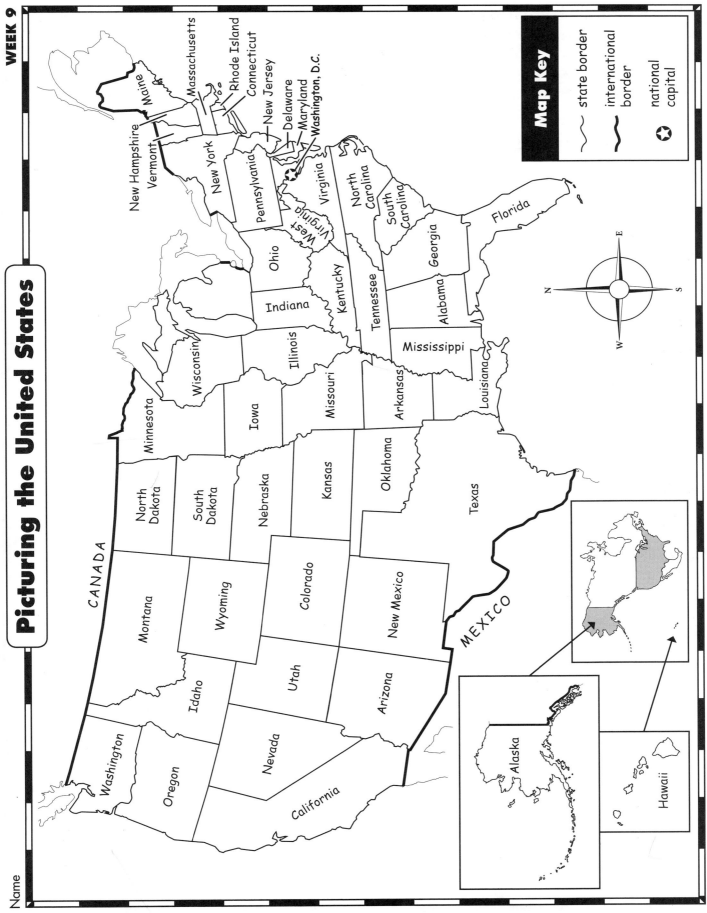

Map Key
- ⌇ state border
- 〜 international border
- ✪ national capital

Maine
New Hampshire
Vermont
Massachusetts
Rhode Island
Connecticut
New Jersey
Delaware
Maryland
Washington, D.C.
New York
Pennsylvania
West Virginia
Virginia
North Carolina
South Carolina
Florida
Ohio
Kentucky
Tennessee
Georgia
Alabama
Indiana
Mississippi
Illinois
Wisconsin
Missouri
Arkansas
Louisiana
Minnesota
Iowa
Oklahoma
Kansas
Texas
North Dakota
South Dakota
Nebraska
Colorado
New Mexico
CANADA
Montana
Wyoming
Utah
Arizona
Idaho
Washington
Oregon
Nevada
California
MEXICO
Alaska
Hawaii

N E S W

Picturing the United States

Monday

1. Does the eastern or western half of the U.S. have larger states?

   _____

2. Where are most of the smallest states found?

   _____

Tuesday

1. Name two states that border the Pacific Ocean.

   _____

2. Which ocean borders the states that are located in the east?

   _____

Wednesday

1. How many states border the Gulf of Mexico?

   _____

2. Which two states are <u>not</u> attached to the rest of the country?

   _____

Picturing the United States

Thursday

1. Which country and which oceans border Alaska?

    _____

2. Are the Hawaiian Islands north, south, east, or west of Alaska?

    _____

Friday

1. Is Canada north or south of the United States?

    _____

2. Is Mexico north or south of the United States?

    _____

Challenge

Close your eyes and picture the map of the United States. On a piece of blank paper, draw a map of the outline shape of the United States. Look at the real map to see how you did.

ANSWER KEY

Monday
1. North America
2. Canada, Mexico, and the United States

Tuesday
1. Canada
2. Mexico

Wednesday
1. Canada
2. Alaska

Thursday
1. 3; Atlantic, Arctic, and Pacific Oceans
2. Belize and Guatemala

Friday
1. Cuba
2. South America

Challenge
Students should follow the directions to make the outline shape of North America. It is not necessary for students to include every little island, as long as they draw the general outline shape of the continent.

Picturing North America

Introducing the Map

Explain to students that a mental map is a map you picture in your mind. Ask students to picture where their classroom is. Have them think about where the office is, the cafeteria, and the library. Tell them the picture they have in their mind is a mental map.

Explain that where one thing is in relation to another is called location. Tell students that when they made a mental map of the school, they were picturing the location of the different rooms in the school.

Show students the map of North America. Talk about the countries on the continent. The students will probably recognize the three large countries of Canada, the United States, and Mexico. Talk about the location of each of these countries in relation to each other.

Show students the seven smaller countries south of Mexico. Students should also notice the islands that are part of North America. There are many islands south of the United States. Also, have students find the island of Greenland. Tell students that there are actually twenty-three countries in North America, but only the largest are labeled on the map.

Then have students look at the small map of the world with North America shaded. Ask students to turn the map page over and picture where North America is in the world and what it looks like. Tell students that what they have just done is to create a mental map of North America.

Now give students a blank piece of paper and have them draw a simple sketch of the shape of North America from memory. Have them compare their map sketch with the actual map. Tell students that making a mental picture of places helps them to understand where different places in the world are located.

Students may find it difficult to understand the concept of mental maps and may need a review each day. Encourage students to try to answer as many questions as possible without looking at the map. Then have students look at the map to check their answers.

Introducing Vocabulary

continent one of the seven largest areas of land on Earth: Africa, Antarctica, Asia, Australia, Europe, North America, or South America

country a part of the world with its own borders and government; nation

location the site or position of something

map sketch a rough drawing of a mental map

mental map a map that a person pictures in his or her mind

Picturing North America

ARCTIC OCEAN

Greenland
(Denmark)

Alaska
(USA)

PACIFIC OCEAN

CANADA

Great Lakes

UNITED STATES

ATLANTIC OCEAN

MEXICO

THE
BAHAMAS

CUBA

DOMINICAN
REPUBLIC

JAMAICA

HAITI

Puerto Rico
(USA)

BELIZE

HONDURAS

CARIBBEAN SEA

NICARAGUA

GUATEMALA

EL
SALVADOR

COSTA RICA

PANAMA

N
W   E
S

Picturing North America

Monday

1. Which continent is shown on the map?

   _____

2. Name the three largest countries on the continent.

   _____

   _____

Tuesday

1. Which large country is north of the United States?

   _____

2. Which large country is south of the United States?

   _____

Wednesday

1. Which large country has lots of islands to the north?

   _____

2. Which U.S. state borders Canada and <u>not</u> the U.S.?

   _____

Picturing North America

Thursday

1. How many oceans border North America? Name them.

   _____

   _____

2. Name the two countries that border southern Mexico.

   _____

Friday

1. Name the largest island country east of Mexico.

   _____

2. Name the continent that is south of North America.

   _____

Challenge

On the map, trace the outline shape of North America in dark red. Place a blank piece of paper over the map. Trace over the lines that show through onto the blank piece of paper. Look at your drawing of North America. Close your eyes and make a mental picture of the shape of North America.

WEEK 11

Daily Geography

Transportation Routes in a Town

Introducing the Map

Explain to students that a route is a way to go from one place to another. Tell students that there are many different types of routes. Discuss different kinds of transportation routes such as streets, highways, bike paths, airport runways, and pedestrian sidewalks.

Ask students to think about a familiar route. Explain to students that a route can be as simple as the way they walk to the mailbox every day. As a class, discuss familiar routes at school. For example, the way to the playground or to the lunch area is a familiar route. Remind students that when they make a picture of a route in their mind they are making a mental map.

Review cardinal and intermediate directions. Explain that people often use directions in order to follow a route. Show students the map of the town. Ask students to name transportation routes shown on the map. They should name things such as streets, a highway, a bike path, and railroad tracks. Remind students that streets can also be called such names as avenues, drives, and ways.

Have students follow the route from the school to the mall, noting the streets and places along the way. Talk about other routes in town to check for understanding.

Introducing Vocabulary

cardinal directions north, south, east, and west (N, S, E, and W)

intermediate directions northeast, northwest, southeast, southwest (NE, NW, SE, SW)

mental map a map that a person pictures in his or her mind

route a way to go from one place to another

transportation how things or people are moved from place to place

---

ANSWER KEY

Monday
1. Any three of the following: bike path, highway, railroad tracks, and streets
2. Highway 60

Tuesday
1. Maple Street
2. around the lake

Wednesday
1. bike path and Boat Drive
2. Forest Avenue

Thursday
1. northwest to southeast or vice versa
2. Pine Street and Maple Street

Friday
1. Pine Street
2. Highway 60

Challenge
Students should color the bike path blue.

Transportation Routes in a Town

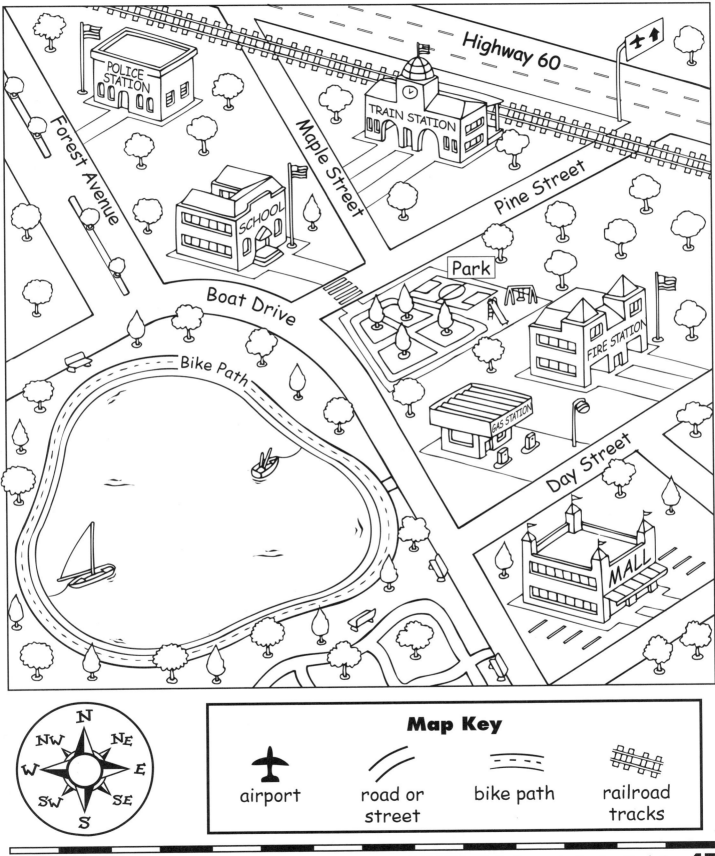

Map Key

airport

road or street

bike path

railroad tracks

Transportation Routes in a Town

Monday

1. Name three kinds of routes that are shown on the map.

   _____

   _____

2. Which highway leads to the airport? _____

Tuesday

1. On which street is the train station?

   _____

2. Does the bike path go around the lake, the school, or the shopping center?

   _____

Wednesday

1. Which two routes are near the lake?

   _____

2. On which street is the entrance to the police station?

   _____

Transportation Routes in a Town

Thursday

1. In which direction do the train tracks run?

   _____

2. Which streets cross the train tracks?

   _____

Friday

1. Which street do you cross to get from the school to the park?

   _____

2. Which route runs alongside the railroad tracks?

   _____

Challenge

Use a blue marker to highlight the bike path on the map.

ANSWER KEY

Monday
1. Interstate Highways 29 and 90
2. U.S. Highways 12, 14, 85, and 281

Tuesday
1. north to south or vice versa
2. U.S. Highway 14

Wednesday
1. east to west or vice versa
2. U.S. Highway 12

Thursday
1. Interstate Highway 90
2. Brookings and Sioux Falls

Friday
1. U.S. Highway 12 and U.S. Highway 281
2. Interstate Highway 90

Challenge
Students should highlight the route of the interstate highways in yellow and the U.S. highways in orange.

A Road Map: South Dakota

Introducing the Map

Explain to students that a route is a way to go from one place to another. Tell students that there are many different types of routes. Discuss different transportation routes such as bike paths, streets and highways, railroad tracks, and pedestrian sidewalks.

Ask students to think about a familiar route. Tell students that a route can be as simple as the way they walk to the mailbox every day. As a class, discuss familiar routes in your town or city. Remind students that when they make a picture of a route in their mind they are making a mental map.

Explain that people often use directions in order to follow a route. Have students look at the road map of South Dakota. Review the symbols in the map key. Explain to students that highways are used for transportation. Tell students that there are two types of highways on the map: an interstate highway and a U.S. highway.

Have students use a finger to follow Interstate 90 across the state, pointing out the cities along the way. Have students notice that the biggest city, Sioux Falls, is at the intersection of Interstates 90 and 29. Explain that an intersection is where two roads meet or cross. Also, have students follow a U.S. highway route.

Introducing Vocabulary

cardinal directions north, south, east, and west (N, S, E, and W)

highway a main road

intersection a place where two or more things meet and cross

mental map a map that a person pictures in his or her mind

route a way to go from one place to another

transportation how things or people are moved from place to place

A Road Map

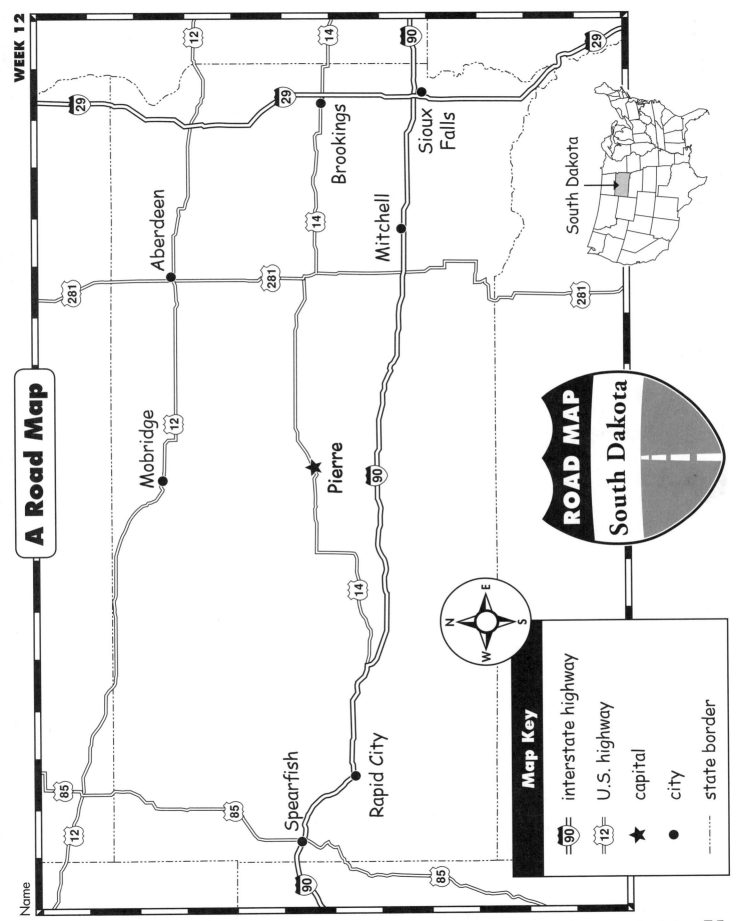

ROAD MAP
South Dakota

South Dakota

Map Key

interstate highway	
U.S. highway	
capital	
city	
state border	

Name

A Road Map: South Dakota

Monday

1. Name the interstate highways shown on the map.

   _____

2. Name the U.S. highways shown on the map.

   _____

Tuesday

1. In which direction does Interstate Highway 29 run?

   _____

2. Which U.S. highway runs through the capital city of Pierre?

   _____

Wednesday

1. In which direction does Interstate Highway 90 run?

   _____

2. Which U.S. highway runs through Mobridge?

   _____

A Road Map: South Dakota

Thursday

1. Which interstate highway runs through the city of Mitchell?

    _____

2. Name the cities along Interstate 29.

    _____

Friday

1. Which U.S. highways intersect in the city of Aberdeen?

    _____

2. Which interstate highway joins U.S. Highway 14?

    _____

Challenge

- Highlight the routes of the interstate highways in yellow.
- Highlight the routes of the U.S. highways in orange.

WEEK 13

Daily Geography

ANSWER KEY

Monday
1. oceans, rivers, lakes, and a gulf
2. 9

Tuesday
1. Colorado, Kansas, Oklahoma, Arkansas
2. Yukon River

Wednesday
1. Atlantic, Arctic (Alaska), and Pacific
2. Washington and Oregon

Thursday
1. Any three of the following: Lake Superior, Lake Huron, Lake Ontario, Lake Michigan, Lake Erie
2. Lake Ontario

Friday
1. Any three of the following: California, Nevada, Arizona, Utah, and Colorado
2. Missouri River, Ohio River, and Arkansas River

Challenge
Students should trace all the rivers in dark blue.
Students should color the Great Lakes light blue.
Students should color the oceans and Gulf of Mexico blue-green.

Waterways of the United States

Introducing the Map

Explain to students that physical features on a map may include: mountains, valleys, plains, oceans, lakes, rivers, and gulfs. Tell students that maps that show these features are called physical maps. Physical maps show the natural landforms and water on Earth's surface.

Show students the map of the waterways of the United States. Explain to students that this physical map only shows the waterways. Talk about the different waterways that are labeled on the map. Have students name the oceans that border the U.S. Define a gulf for students and talk about the Gulf of Mexico.

Next, name the rivers on the map. Point out that many rivers run through more than one state. Have students trace the route of the Mississippi River with their fingers. Then talk about the lakes. Tell students that the five largest lakes are called the "Great Lakes." Have students locate and name them. Help students notice that they form a border between the U.S. and Canada.

Point out the small maps of Alaska and Hawaii. Discuss the locations of Alaska and Hawaii and the waterways that are included. Remind students that there are many lakes and rivers in the U.S. This map only shows a sampling of them.

Introducing Vocabulary

Great Lakes five freshwater lakes: Superior, Michigan, Huron, Erie, and Ontario

gulf a large area of ocean partly surrounded by land; larger than a bay

lake a large body of fresh water surrounded by land

landform a natural feature on Earth's surface, like a mountain or hill

ocean a large body of salt water

physical feature a natural part of Earth such as a mountain or an ocean

physical map a map that shows natural landforms and water

river a large stream that flows into a larger river, lake, sea, or ocean

state a group of people united under one government; a state can be a whole country or part of a country, such as the United States

waterway a river, ocean, or other body of water on which boats or ships travel

Waterways of the United States

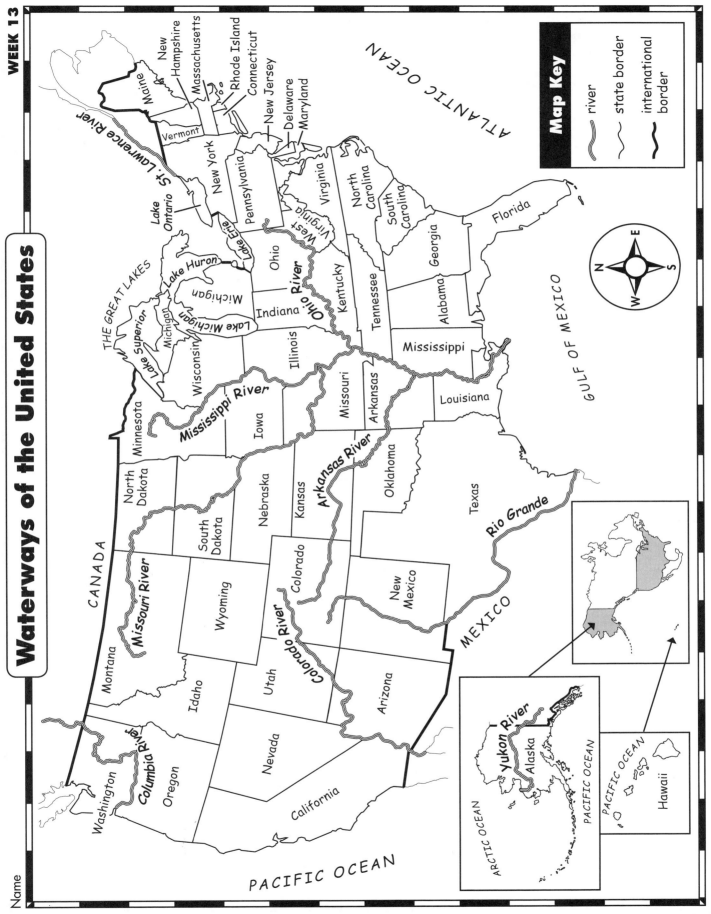

Map Key

- ∿ river
- ⌇ state border
- ⌇ international border

THE GREAT LAKES

Lake Superior
Lake Michigan
Lake Huron
Lake Erie
Lake Ontario

St. Lawrence River

ATLANTIC OCEAN

GULF OF MEXICO

Mississippi River

Missouri River

Arkansas River

Colorado River

Columbia River

Rio Grande

Ohio River

Yukon River

ARCTIC OCEAN

PACIFIC OCEAN

CANADA

MEXICO

PACIFIC OCEAN

Name

Waterways of the United States

Monday

1. Which four kinds of waterways are shown on the map?

   _____

   _____

2. How many rivers are shown on the map? _____

Tuesday

1. Which states does the Arkansas River run through?

   _____

   _____

2. Which river runs through Alaska?

   _____

Wednesday

1. Name the oceans that border the U.S.

   _____

2. Which two states share the Columbia River?

   _____

Waterways of the United States

Thursday

1. Name three of the Great Lakes.

_____

_____

2. The St. Lawrence River flows out of which lake?

_____

Friday

1. Name three of the states that share the Colorado River.

_____

2. Which three rivers on this map flow into the Mississippi River?

_____

Challenge

- Trace all the rivers in dark blue.
- Color the Great Lakes light blue.
- Color the oceans and the Gulf of Mexico blue-green.

ANSWER KEY

Monday
1. Rocky Mountains
2. plains or Great Plains

Tuesday
1. 5
2. Rio Grande

Wednesday
1. 2
2. Mount Elbert; 14,433 feet (4,399 m) high.

Thursday
1. west
2. South Platte River

Friday
1. snow ski
2. wheat fields

Challenge
Students should add trees in the western half of the state. On the map key, students should add a tree to represent a forest.

A Physical Map: Colorado

Introducing the Map

Share with students that physical features on a map may include: mountains, valleys, plains, oceans, lakes, rivers, and gulfs. Tell students that maps that show these features are called physical maps. Physical maps show the natural landforms and water on Earth's surface. Discuss that a physical map might show a small area such as a park, or larger areas such as states, regions, or countries.

Show students the physical map of the state of Colorado. Discuss the physical features and the symbols that represent them. Tell students that Colorado is in the heart of the Rocky Mountains. The Rockies are the longest mountain system in North America. Share with students that there are between 50 and 60 peaks that reach 14,000 feet (4,279 m) or more. Mount Elbert is the highest peak in Colorado. Another famous peak is called Pikes Peak. The mountains are rich in gold, silver, lead, and iron. The mountains are also famous for mountain climbing and snow skiing.

Point out that the eastern part of the state is made up of plains called the Great Plains. Herds of cattle and sheep graze on the plains. There are many wheat and cornfields on the plains.

Share with students that there are important rivers in Colorado. Name the rivers on the map and tell students that seven western states get their water from the Colorado River.

Show students Colorado's location on the small map of the United States. Remind students that only a sampling of landforms and waterways are shown on the map.

Introducing Vocabulary

landform a natural feature on Earth's surface, like a mountain or hill

mountain a piece of land that has steep sides and a round or pointed peak; higher than a hill

mountain peak the highest point of a mountain

mountain range a group or chain of mountains

physical feature a natural part of Earth such as a mountain or an ocean

physical map a map that shows natural landforms and water

plains a large flat area of land

river a large stream that flows into a larger river, lake, sea, or ocean

state a group of people united under one government; a state can be a whole country or part of a country, such as the United States

Name

A Physical Map: Colorado

Colorado has more than 50 tall mountain peaks. Mount Elbert is the highest. It is 14,433 feet (4,399 m) high.

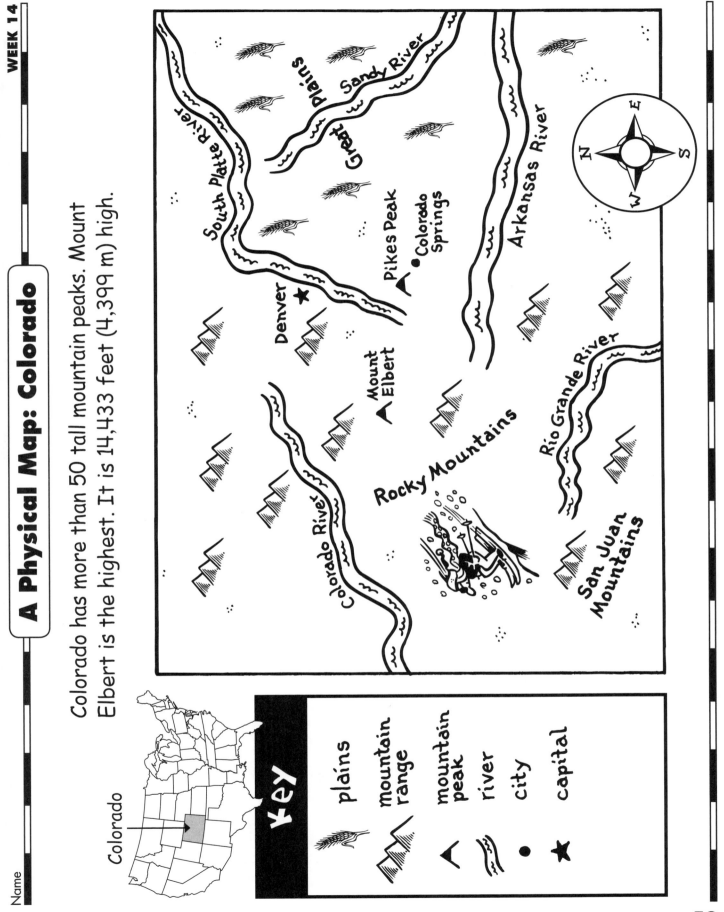

Colorado

Key

plains	🌾
mountain range	⛰
mountain peak	◣
river	〰
city	●
capital	★

A Physical Map: Colorado

Monday

1. Name the large mountain range in Colorado.

   _____

2. Which landform is in the eastern part of Colorado?

   _____

Tuesday

1. How many rivers are shown on the map?

   _____

2. Which river is found in southern Colorado?

   _____

Wednesday

1. How many tall mountain peaks are shown on the map?

   _____

2. Which mountain peak is the highest? How high is it?

   _____

   _____

Daily Geography

A Physical Map: Colorado

WEEK 14

Thursday

1. Are the Rocky Mountains east or west of the capital?

   _____

2. Which river runs through the northeast part of Colorado?

   _____

Friday

1. Which activity would people most likely do in the Rocky Mountains—snow ski or water ski?

   _____

2. Which is most likely found in the Great Plains—wheat fields or gold mines?

   _____

Challenge

Colorado has 12 national forests. They are mostly in the western half of the state. On the map, draw several trees west of Denver. Draw a picture of a tree and write the word **forest** in the map key.

ANSWER KEY

Monday
1. desert, mountain, canyon
2. Gila River

Tuesday
1. the Grand Canyon
2. northeast

Wednesday
1. Sonoran Desert
2. Painted Desert

Thursday
1. northwest Arizona
2. the Colorado River

Friday
1. The Grand Canyon State
2. Any of the following: California, Nevada, New Mexico, Utah, Wyoming, or the country of Mexico

Challenge
Students should color the Grand Canyon and the Painted Desert in shades of yellow, brown, red, and pink.

A Physical Map: Arizona

Introducing the Map

Share with students that physical features on a map may include: mountains, valleys, plains, oceans, lakes, rivers, and gulfs. Tell students that maps that show these features are called physical maps. Physical maps show the natural landforms and water on Earth's surface. Discuss that a physical map might show a small area such as a park, or larger areas such as states, regions, or countries.

Show students the physical map of the state of Arizona. Discuss the physical features and the symbols that represent them. A plateau of high flat land covers most of northern Arizona. Millions of years ago, rushing water of the Colorado River cut through the layers of rock and formed the Grand Canyon. The Grand Canyon is one of the largest canyons in the world. The walls of the canyon have different shades and colors. People from all over the world come to see the colorful Grand Canyon. Read the caption on the map page to review its dimensions. Humphreys Peak, the highest point in Arizona, is also located in this high plateau, near Flagstaff.

Talk about the deserts of Arizona. The Painted Desert in northeastern Arizona is known for its colorful rock formations. The Sonoran Desert in southern Arizona is hot and dry, but it also gets short periods of heavy rains. Giant saguaro cactus plants grow there. The desert consists of gravel-covered plains, rocky hills and mountains, and dry lakes and riverbeds.

Be sure to read the names of the rivers on the map. Point out Arizona's location on the small map of the United States. Remind students that only a sampling of physical features has been included on the map of Arizona.

Introducing Vocabulary

canyon a deep, narrow valley with steep sides

desert dry, sandy land that gets little or no rain

mountain a piece of land that has steep sides and a round or pointed peak; higher than a hill

physical feature a natural part of Earth such as a mountain or an ocean

physical map a map that shows natural landforms and water

plateau high flat land; sometimes called a tableland

river a large stream that flows into a larger river, lake, sea, or ocean

state a group of people united under one government; a state can be a whole country or part of a country, such as the United States

Name

A Physical Map: Arizona

Arizona is known as the "Grand Canyon State." The Grand Canyon is 277 miles (443 km) long. It is 15 miles (24 km) wide. The canyon is more than a mile (1.6 km) deep. The Colorado River runs along the base of the canyon.

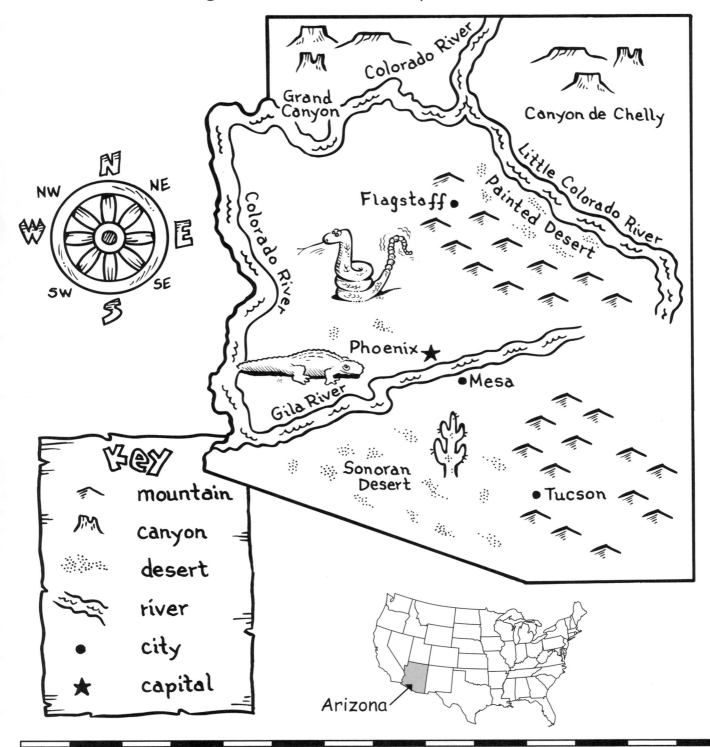

A Physical Map: Arizona

Monday

1. Name three kinds of landforms in Arizona.

   _____

2. Which river runs by the capital city of Phoenix?

   _____

Tuesday

1. What is the name of the most famous canyon in Arizona?

   _____

2. In which part of Arizona is Canyon de Chelly?

   _____

Wednesday

1. Which desert is south of the Gila River?

   _____

2. Which desert is located south of the Little Colorado River?

   _____

A Physical Map: Arizona

Thursday

1. In which part of the state is the Grand Canyon located?

   _____

2. Which river lies at the base of the Grand Canyon?

   _____

Friday

1. What is Arizona's nickname?

   _____

2. Name a state or country that borders Arizona.

   _____

Challenge

The Grand Canyon and the Painted Desert are very colorful. Color the Grand Canyon the Painted Desert in shades of yellow, brown, red, and pink.

Daily Geography

ANSWER KEY

Monday
1. Any two of the following: Lake Itasca, Lake of the Woods, Lake Superior, Leech Lake, Lower and Upper Red Lakes, and Mille Lacs Lake
2. Any two of the following: Minnesota River, Mississippi River, Red River, and St. Croix River

Tuesday
1. Lake Itasca
2. north and south

Wednesday
1. Gooseberry Falls
2. Canada

Thursday
1. Lake Superior
2. Mille Lacs Lake

Friday
1. The Red River is on the western border of Minnesota.
2. Land of 10,000 Lakes

Challenge
Students should color all the lakes on the map light blue and trace the rivers in dark blue.

A Physical Map: Minnesota

Introducing the Map

Share with students that physical features on a map may include: mountains, valleys, plains, oceans, lakes, rivers, and waterfalls. Tell students that maps that show these features are called physical maps. Physical maps show the natural landforms and water on Earth's surface. Discuss that a physical map might show a small area such as a park, or larger areas such as states, regions, or countries.

Show students the physical map of the state of Minnesota. Discuss the physical features and the symbols that represent them. Explain to students that millions of years ago large glaciers covered Minnesota. The glaciers moved across the land and flattened it into plains. Explain to students that the glaciers were so big that when they began to melt they created many lakes. Because of this, Minnesota has thousands of clear blue lakes. Have students name the lakes that are labeled on the map. Share with students that Lake Superior, the largest of the Great Lakes, borders Minnesota. Be sure to read the caption to students.

Tell students that Lake Itasca is where the Mississippi River begins. Remind students that the Mississippi River flows from Minnesota, south to the Gulf of Mexico. Have students locate other rivers and waterfalls on the map.

Point out Minnesota's location on the small map of the United States. Remind students that only a sampling of the thousands of lakes has been included on this map.

Introducing Vocabulary

glacier a large mass of ice

lake a large body of fresh water surrounded by land

physical feature a natural part of Earth such as a mountain or an ocean

physical map a map that shows natural landforms and water

plains a large flat area of land

river a large stream that flows into a larger river, lake, sea, or ocean

state a group of people united under one government; a state can be a whole country or part of a country, such as the United States

waterfall a natural stream of water falling from a high place

A Physical Map: Minnesota

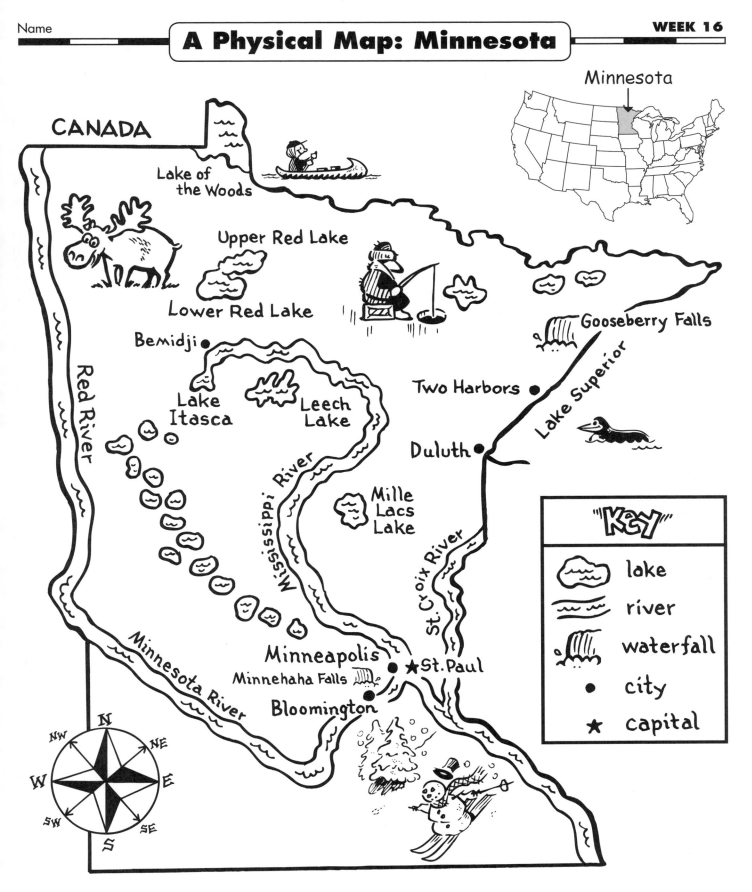

Minnesota

CANADA

Lake of the Woods

Upper Red Lake

Lower Red Lake

Bemidji

Red River

Lake Itasca

Leech Lake

Gooseberry Falls

Two Harbors

Lake Superior

Duluth

Mississippi River

Mille Lacs Lake

St. Croix River

Minnesota River

Minneapolis

Minnehaha Falls

Bloomington

St. Paul

"Key"

〰 lake

〰 river

waterfall

• city

★ capital

N NE E SE S SW W NW

Minnesota is known as the "Land of 10,000 Lakes."

A Physical Map: Minnesota

Monday

1. Name two of the lakes on the map.

   _____

2. Name two of the rivers on the map.

   _____

Tuesday

1. The Mississippi River begins at which lake?

   _____

2. Does the Mississippi River run north and south, or east and west?

   _____

Wednesday

1. Which waterfall is located near Two Harbors?

   _____

2. Lake of the Woods is between Minnesota and which country?

   _____

A Physical Map: Minnesota

Thursday

1. Which large lake borders northeast Minnesota?

   _____

2. Which lake is between the Mississippi and St. Croix Rivers?

   _____

Friday

1. Where is the Red River located?

   _____

   _____

2. What is Minnesota's nickname?

   _____

Challenge

Color all the lakes on the map light blue. Trace all the rivers in dark blue.

WEEK 17

Daily Geography

A Physical Map: Massachusetts

Introducing the Map

Share with students that physical features on a map may include: mountains, valleys, plains, islands, oceans, lakes, and rivers. Tell students that maps that show these features are called physical maps. Physical maps show the natural landforms and water on Earth's surface. Discuss that a physical map might show a small area such as a park, or larger areas such as states, regions, or countries.

Show students the physical map of the state of Massachusetts. Discuss the physical features and the symbols that represent them. Note that the physical features highlighted in this lesson are mostly located along the rugged coastline of Massachusetts.

Explain to students that a bay is a part of an ocean or lake partly enclosed by the coastline. Point out the islands off Massachusetts. Explain that Nantucket Sound is the area of water located between the mainland and the islands. Discuss the definition of a *sound*.

Review the definitions of the vocabulary words throughout the week. Remind students that only a sampling of physical features has been included on the map.

ANSWER KEY

Monday
1. Atlantic Ocean
2. Massachusetts Bay, Cape Cod Bay, and Buzzards Bay

Tuesday
1. Martha's Vineyard and Nantucket
2. Boston; Massachusetts Bay

Wednesday
1. Merrimack River and Charles River
2. Connecticut River and the Housatonic River

Thursday
1. Cape Cod Peninsula
2. Provincetown

Friday
1. The coastline is rugged with lots of bays and a large peninsula that juts out into the Atlantic Ocean.
2. Nantucket Sound

Challenge
Students should color the coastline of Massachusetts brown, trace the rivers in dark blue, and color the Atlantic Ocean with its bays and sound light blue.

Introducing Vocabulary

bay an area of ocean or lake partly surrounded by land; smaller than a gulf

coast land that is next to an ocean or sea

coastline the place where the land and the ocean meet; the outline of the coast

harbor a sheltered body of water where ships anchor

island an area of land surrounded by water

peninsula a piece of land that sticks out and is mostly surrounded by water

physical feature a natural part of Earth such as a mountain or an ocean

physical map a map that shows natural landforms and water

sound a wide channel that connects two large bodies of water

state a group of people united under one government; a state can be a whole country or part of a country, such as the United States

Name _____

A Physical Map: Massachusetts

Massachusetts has a rugged coastline. Ships anchor in the safe harbors along the bays.

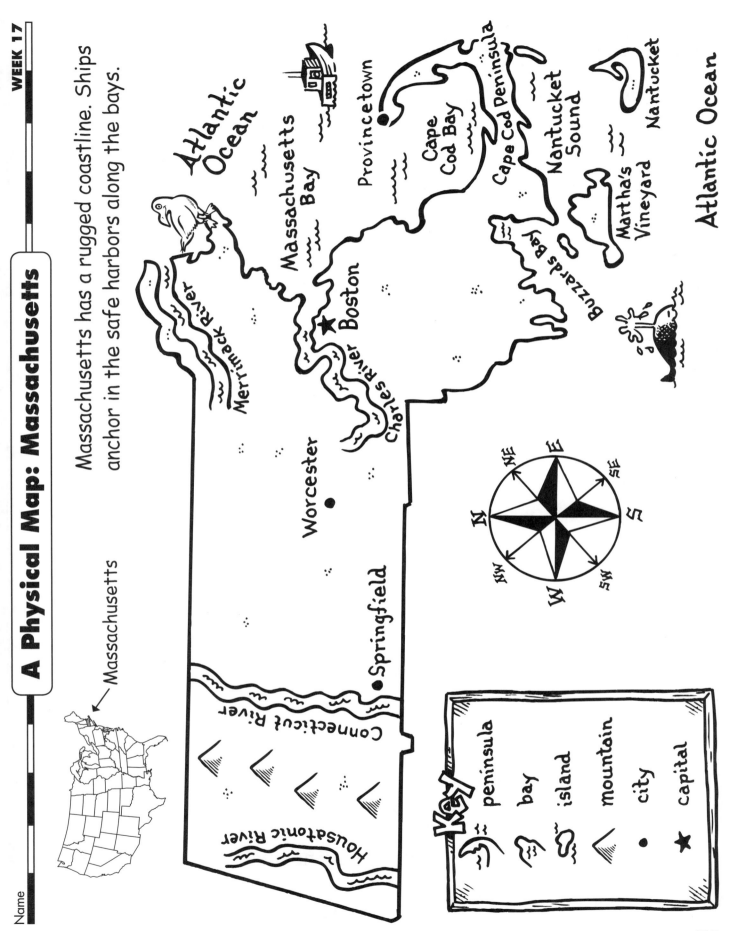

Massachusetts

Atlantic Ocean

Merrimack River

Atlantic Ocean

Massachusetts Bay

Provincetown

Cape Cod Bay

Cape Cod Peninsula

Nantucket Sound

Nantucket

Martha's Vineyard

Buzzards Bay

Atlantic Ocean

Boston

Charles River

Worcester

Springfield

Connecticut River

Housatonic River

NE E SE
N   S
NW W SW

Key
~~ peninsula
bay
island
mountain
• city
★ capital

A Physical Map: Massachusetts

Monday

1. Which ocean borders Massachusetts?

   _____

2. Which three bays are shown on this map?

   _____

   _____

Tuesday

1. Which two islands are named on this map?

   _____

2. What is the capital of Massachusetts? Which bay is near the capital city?

   _____

Wednesday

1. Which two rivers flow into the Atlantic Ocean?

   _____

2. Which two rivers are separated by mountains?

   _____

A Physical Map: Massachusetts

Thursday

1. Name the peninsula on this map.

   _____

2. Name the city located at the tip of the peninsula.

   _____

   _____

Friday

1. What is the coastline of Massachusetts like?

   _____

   _____

2. Which waterway is between Cape Cod and Martha's Vineyard?

   _____

Challenge

On the map page, color the coastline of Massachusetts brown. Trace the rivers in dark blue. Color the Atlantic Ocean with its bays and sound light blue.

A Physical Map: Hawaii

Introducing the Map

Share with students that physical features on a map may include: mountains, valleys, plains, islands, oceans, lakes, and volcanoes. Tell students that maps that show these features are called physical maps. Physical maps show the natural landforms and water on Earth's surface. Discuss that a physical map might show a small area such as a park, or larger areas such as states, regions, or countries.

Show students the physical map of the state of Hawaii. Tell students that the physical features that will be highlighted this week are islands, mountains, and volcanoes. Explain to students that Hawaii is the only state that is not located in North America. Hawaii is a chain of volcanic islands that is 2,400 miles (3,860 km) southwest of the mainland of the United States. Hawaii is actually made up of 132 islands, but most of them are too tiny for people to live on. The eight largest islands are called the main islands of Hawaii.

Explain to students that the Hawaiian Islands were formed by the eruption of undersea volcanoes. The volcanic mountains that created the Hawaiian Islands are among the greatest mountain ranges on Earth. Most of the volcanoes are no longer active, but some continue to erupt. The most active volcano is on the "Big Island," or Hawaii. It is called Kilauea. Since 1952, this volcano has erupted 34 times. Since 1983, Kilauea has continually erupted along the eastern rim. The eruptions have added 544 acres of lava and black sand beaches to the big island. Mauna Loa is the highest volcanic mountain in the state. It erupts about every four years.

Be sure to help students pronounce the names of the islands and review the vocabulary throughout the week. Remind students there are other active volcanoes in Hawaii, but only two were highlighted on this map.

Introducing Vocabulary

island an area of land surrounded by water

mountain a piece of land that has steep sides and a round or pointed peak; higher than a hill

mountain range a group or chain of mountains

state a group of people united under one government; a state can be a whole country or part of a country, such as the United States

volcano an opening in the Earth's surface where lava, gases and ashes are forced out

ANSWER KEY

Monday
1. 132; 8
2. the Pacific Ocean

Tuesday
1. Honolulu; Oahu
2. Hawaii or the "Big Island"

Wednesday
1. Kahoolawe, Lanai, and Molokai
2. Kahoolawe

Thursday
1. southwest
2. 2,400 miles (3,860 km)

Friday
1. 2; 5
2. Kilauea and Mauna Loa; Kilauea

Challenge
A volcano is an opening in the Earth's surface where lava, gases, and ashes are forced out. Drawing should show a volcano erupting.

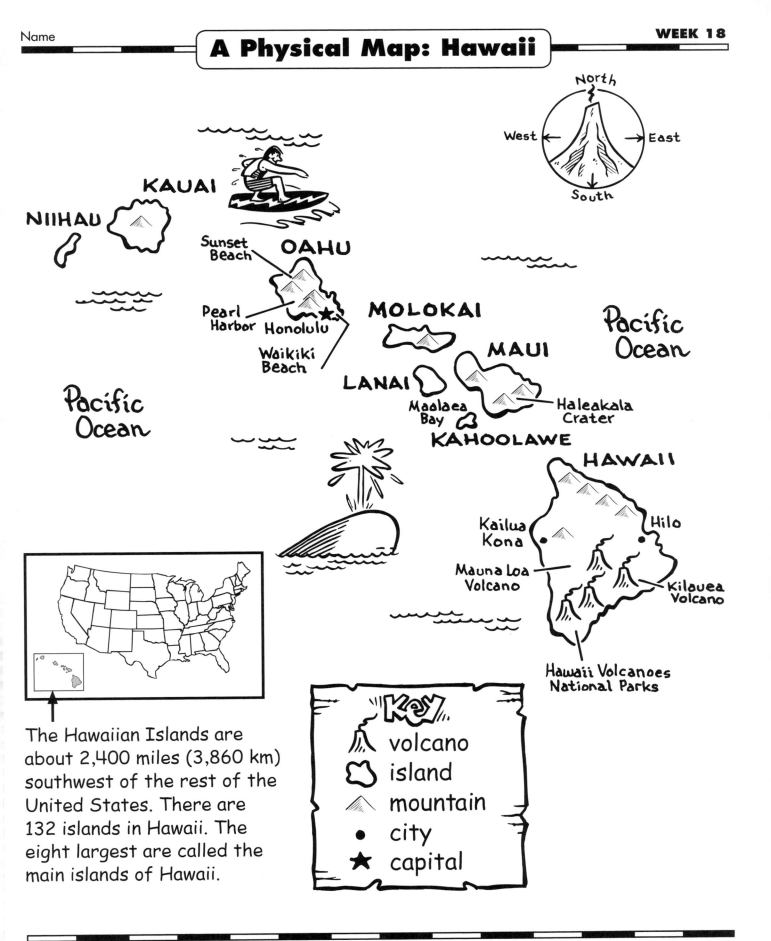

North

West ← → East

South

KAUAI

NIIHAU

Sunset Beach

OAHU

Pearl Harbor   Honolulu

Waikiki Beach

MOLOKAI

Pacific Ocean

MAUI

LANAI

Maalaea Bay

Haleakala Crater

Pacific Ocean

KAHOOLAWE

HAWAII

Kailua Kona

Hilo

Mauna Loa Volcano

Kilauea Volcano

Hawaii Volcanoes National Parks

The Hawaiian Islands are about 2,400 miles (3,860 km) southwest of the rest of the United States. There are 132 islands in Hawaii. The eight largest are called the main islands of Hawaii.

Key

volcano
island
mountain
• city
★ capital

A Physical Map: Hawaii

Monday

1. Hawaii is made up of how many islands? How many main islands are there?

   _____

2. In which ocean is Hawaii located? _____

Tuesday

1. What is the capital of Hawaii? On which island is the capital found?

   _____

2. What is the name of the largest island in size?

   _____

Wednesday

1. Which three islands are closest to Maui?

   _____

   _____

2. Which main island is smallest in size?

   _____

A Physical Map: Hawaii

Thursday

1. In which direction is Hawaii from the mainland of the U.S.?

   _____

2. How far away is the state of Hawaii from the mainland of the U.S.?

   _____

Friday

1. How many main islands are northwest of Oahu? How many main islands are southeast of Oahu?

   _____

2. Name the two volcanoes on the map. Which one is the most active?

   _____

Challenge

On the map page, write the definition of a volcano. Draw a picture of a volcano erupting. Use a picture dictionary to help you.

WEEK 19

The Pacific Region of the United States

Introducing the Map

Explain to students that political maps show human-made features on the Earth. These features may include borders between states, cities, towns, neighborhoods, roadways, and other places or things that humans have put on Earth.

Introduce the term *region*. Explain to students that a region is a large area that has common features. Tell students that the United States is divided into six political regions. They are the Pacific, Rocky Mountain, Southwest, North-Central, Southeast, and the Northeast regions. Each region is made up of a group of states that have certain common characteristics that make it different from other areas. Examples of common features that a region of the United States may have are similar physical features or similar weather patterns. The name of the region is also given because of the similar location of the states within the country.

Show students the map of the Pacific region of the United States. Point out that the Pacific region includes the states of Washington, Oregon, California, Alaska, and Hawaii. Tell students to look at the small map of the United States. Point out the shaded Pacific region on the small map.

Ask students why Washington, Oregon, California, Alaska, and Hawaii are called the Pacific Region. Students should recognize that all the states border the geographic feature of the Pacific Ocean. They are also the states located the farthest west in the United States.

Please note that other regions of the United States are included in Weeks 20, 21, 22, and 25.

Introducing Vocabulary

border a line on a map showing the edge of a city, state, or country

capital a city where the government of a country or state is located

human-made feature a part of Earth such as a city or a road created by people

political map a map that shows human-made features

region a large area with common features

state a group of people united under one government; a state can be a whole country or part of a country, such as the United States

ANSWER KEY

Monday
1. 5
2. the Pacific Ocean

Tuesday
1. California, Oregon, and Washington
2. Hawaii

Wednesday
1. California and Washington
2. Washington and Oregon

Thursday
1. Alaska and Washington
2. California

Friday
1. Alaska; Arctic and Pacific Oceans
2. Alaska; Hawaii

Challenge
Part 1

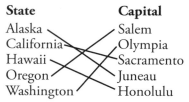

State	Capital
Alaska	Salem
California	Olympia
Hawaii	Sacramento
Oregon	Juneau
Washington	Honolulu

Part 2
Students should write the names of the capitals next to the stars on the states.

The Pacific Region of the United States

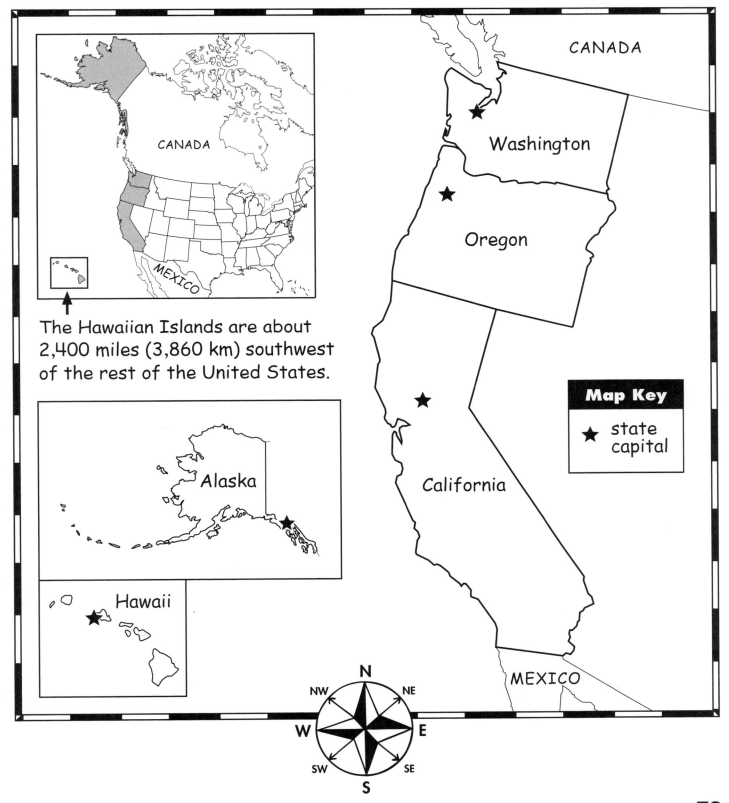

The Hawaiian Islands are about 2,400 miles (3,860 km) southwest of the rest of the United States.

CANADA

Washington

Oregon

California

MEXICO

Map Key

★ state capital

Alaska

Hawaii

N
NW — NE
W — E
SW — SE
S

The Pacific Region of the United States

Monday

1. How many states are in the Pacific Region?

   _____

2. Which ocean do all the states border?

   _____

Tuesday

1. Which three states are on the mainland of the U.S.?

   _____

2. Which state is made up of all islands?

   _____

Wednesday

1. Which states share a border with Oregon?

   _____

2. Which states are north of California?

   _____

The Pacific Region of the United States

Thursday

1. Which states border Canada?

   _____

2. Which state borders Mexico? _____

Friday

1. Which state is the largest in land area? Which two oceans border the state?

   _____

2. Which state is farthest north? Which state is farthest south?

   _____

Challenge

Part 1: Draw a line from the state to its capital. The first one has been completed for you. Use a United States map to help you.

State	Capital
Alaska	Salem
California	Olympia
Hawaii	Sacramento
Oregon	Juneau
Washington	Honolulu

Part 2: On the map, write the name of each capital next to the star on each state.

WEEK 20

ANSWER KEY

Monday
1. 4
2. Arizona, New Mexico, Oklahoma, and Texas

Tuesday
1. Texas
2. Mexico

Wednesday
1. New Mexico and Texas
2. Oklahoma

Thursday
1. Texas
2. Arizona

Friday
1. The states of New Mexico and Oklahoma, the country of Mexico, and the Gulf of Mexico all border Texas.
2. The four states are located in the same area called the Southwest region.

Challenge
Part 1

State	Capital
Arizona	Oklahoma City
New Mexico	Phoenix
Oklahoma	Austin
Texas	Santa Fe

Part 2
Students should write the names of the capitals next to the stars on the states.

The Southwest Region of the United States

Introducing the Map

Explain to students that political maps show human-made features on the Earth. These features may include borders between states, cities, towns, neighborhoods, roadways, and other places or things that humans have put on Earth.

Introduce the term *region*. Explain to students that a region is a large area that has common features. Tell students that the United States is divided into six political regions. They are the Pacific, Rocky Mountain, Southwest, North-Central, Southeast, and the Northeast regions. Each region is made up of a group of states that have certain common characteristics that make it different from other areas. Examples of common features that a region of the United States may have are similar physical features or similar weather patterns. The name of the region is given because of the approximate geographic location of the states within the country.

Show students the map of the Southwest region of the United States. Point out that the Southwest region includes the states of Arizona, New Mexico, Texas, and Oklahoma. Tell students to look at the small map of the United States. Point out the shaded Southwest region on the small map.

Ask students why the states of Arizona, New Mexico, Texas, and Oklahoma are called the Southwest region. Students may recognize that all the states are located in the southwest part of the United States.

Please note that other regions of the United States are included in Weeks 19, 21, 22, and 25.

Introducing Vocabulary

border a line on a map showing the edge of a city, state, or country

capital a city where the government of a country or state is located

human-made feature a part of Earth such as a city or a road created by people

political map a map that shows human-made features

region a large area with common features

state a group of people united under one government; a state can be a whole country or part of a country, such as the United States

The Southwest Region of the United States

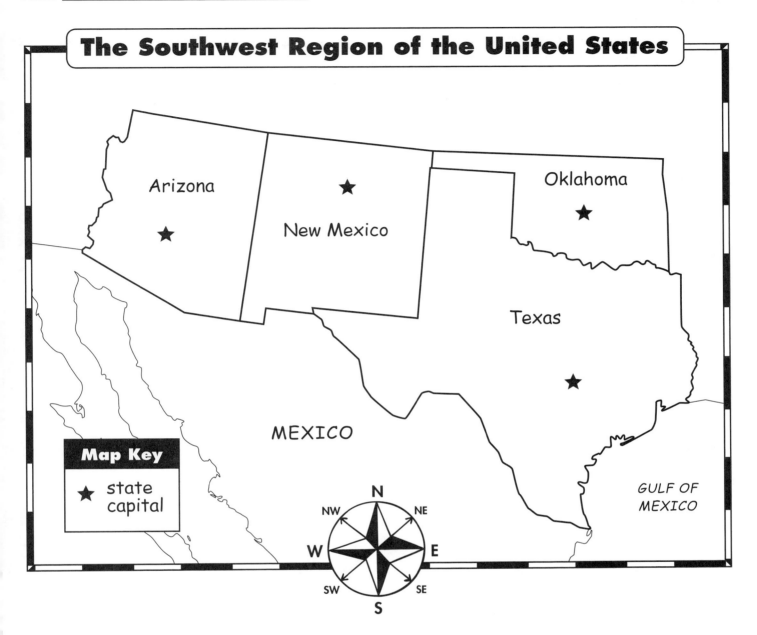

Arizona ★

New Mexico ★

Oklahoma ★

Texas ★

MEXICO

GULF OF MEXICO

Map Key

★ state capital

N
NW   NE
W   E
SW   SE
S

CANADA

PACIFIC OCEAN

ATLANTIC OCEAN

MEXICO

Gulf of Mexico

The Southwest Region of the United States

Monday

1. How many states are in the Southwest region?

   _____

2. Which states are in the Southwest region?

   _____

   _____

Tuesday

1. Which state is the largest in size?

   _____

2. Are the southwest states closer to Canada or Mexico?

   _____

Wednesday

1. Which southwest states border Oklahoma?

   _____

2. Which southwest state does <u>not</u> share a border with Mexico?

   _____

Daily Geography

WEEK 20

The Southwest Region of the United States

Thursday

1. Which state has the longest border with Mexico? _____

2. Which state borders California, New Mexico, Nevada, and Utah?

   _____

Friday

1. Name all the borders of Texas that are labeled on the map.

   _____

   _____

2. Why are Arizona, New Mexico, Oklahoma, and Texas called a region?

   _____

Challenge

Part 1: Draw a line from the state to its capital. The first one has been completed for you. Use a United States map to help you.

State	Capital
Arizona	Oklahoma City
New Mexico	Phoenix
Oklahoma	Austin
Texas	Santa Fe

Part 2: On the map, write the name of each capital next to the star on each state.

WEEK 21

Daily Geography

ANSWER KEY

Monday
1. 9
2. Maine, New York, and Pennsylvania

Tuesday
1. the Atlantic Ocean
2. Canada

Wednesday
1. New Jersey and New York
2. New York

Thursday
1. Rhode Island
2. Maine

Friday
1. Any three of the following: Connecticut, Rhode Island, New York, Vermont, or New Hampshire
2. Any three of the following: Maine, New Hampshire, Massachusetts, Rhode Island, Connecticut, or New Jersey, or New York

Challenge

Part 1
1. d
2. c
3. h
4. f
5. i
6. a
7. b
8. g
9. e

Part 2
Students should write the names of the capitals next to the stars on the states.

The Northeast Region of the United States

Introducing the Map

Explain to students that political maps show human-made features on the Earth. These features may include borders between states, cities, towns, neighborhoods, roadways, and other places or things that humans have put on Earth.

Introduce the term region. Explain to students that a region is a large area that has common features. Tell students that the United States is divided into six political regions. They are the Pacific, Rocky Mountain, Southwest, North-Central, Southeast, and the Northeast regions. Each region is made up of a group of states that have certain common characteristics that make it different from other areas. Examples of common features that a region of the United States may have are similar physical features or similar weather patterns. Or the name of the region is given because of the similar location of the states within the country.

Show students the map of the Northeast region of the United States. Point out that the Northeast region includes the states of Maine, New Hampshire Vermont, Massachusetts, Connecticut, Rhode Island, New Jersey, Pennsylvania, and New York. Tell students to look at the small map of the United States. Point out the shaded Northeast region on the small map.

Ask students why the states of Maine, New Hampshire, Vermont, Massachusetts, Connecticut, Rhode Island, New Jersey, Pennsylvania, and New York are called the Northeast region. Students may recognize that all the states are located in the northeast part of the United States. Explain that the Northeast states are small in size but large in population. A lot of people live in the Northeast states. For example, more than eight million people live in New York City.

You may wish to extend the lesson to discuss how the Northeast is sometimes divided into two smaller regions called New England and the Mid-Atlantic states. New England includes Connecticut, Maine, Massachusetts, New Hampshire, Rhode Island, and Vermont. The Mid-Atlantic states are New Jersey, New York, and Pennsylvania.

Note that other regions of the United States are included in Weeks 19, 20, 22, and 25.

Introducing Vocabulary

border a line on a map showing the edge of a city, state or country

capital a city where the government of a country or state is located

human-made feature a part of Earth such as a city or a road created by people

political map a map that shows human-made features

region a large area with common features

state a group of people united under one government; a state can be a whole country or part of a country such as the United States

The Northeast Region of the United States

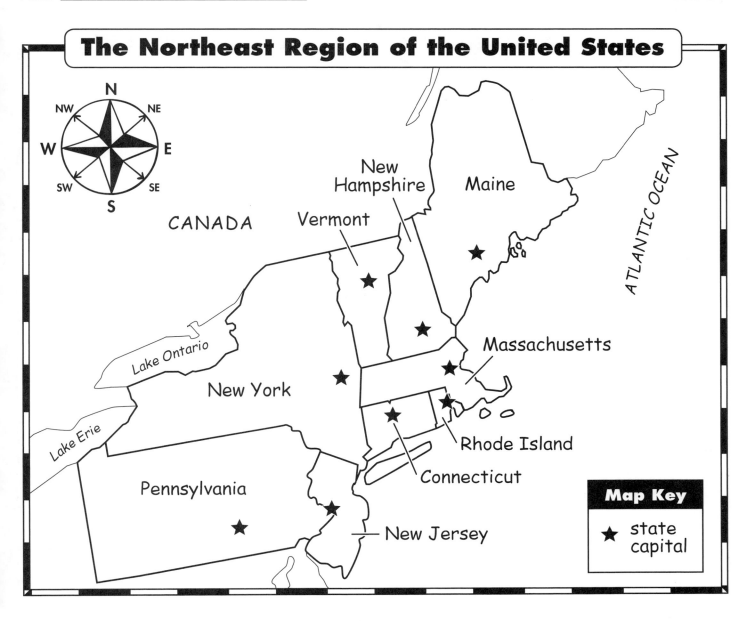

N
NW   NE
W   E
SW   SE
S

CANADA

ATLANTIC OCEAN

New Hampshire
Maine
Vermont

Lake Ontario

New York

Massachusetts

Lake Erie

Pennsylvania

Rhode Island

Connecticut

New Jersey

Map Key

★ state capital

CANADA

PACIFIC OCEAN

ATLANTIC OCEAN

MEXICO

Gulf of Mexico

The Northeast Region of the United States

Monday

1. How many states are in the Northeast region?

   _____

2. Name the three largest states in size.

   _____

Tuesday

1. Which ocean borders six of the states in the Northeast region?

   _____

2. Which country is north of the Northeast region of the U.S.?

   _____

Wednesday

1. Pennsylvania borders which states in the Northeast?

   _____

2. Which state borders both Lake Erie and Lake Ontario?

   _____

The Northeast Region of the United States

Thursday

1. Which state is the smallest in size? _____

2. Which state borders Canada and only one U.S. state?

   _____

Friday

1. Name three of the five states that border Massachusetts.

   _____

2. Name three states that border the Atlantic Ocean.

   _____

Challenge

Part 1: Match each capital with each state. The first three have been completed for you. Use a United States map to help you name the others.

State		**Capital**
1. Connecticut	_d_	a. Albany
2. Maine	_c_	b. Harrisburg
3. Massachusetts	_h_	c. Augusta
4. New Hampshire	____	d. Hartford
5. New Jersey	____	e. Montpelier
6. New York	____	f. Concord
7. Pennsylvania	____	g. Providence
8. Rhode Island	____	h. Boston
9. Vermont	____	i. Trenton

Part 2: On the map, write the name of each capital next to the star on each state.

The Southeast Region of the United States

Introducing the Map

Explain to students that political maps show human-made features on the Earth. These features may include borders between states, cities, towns, neighborhoods, roadways, and other places or things that humans have put on Earth.

Introduce the term *region*. Explain to students that a region is a large area that has common features. Tell students that the United States is divided into six political regions. They are the Pacific, Rocky Mountain, Southwest, North-Central, Southeast, and the Northeast regions. Each region is made up of a group of states that have certain common characteristics that make it different from other areas. Examples of common features that a region of the United States may have are similar physical features or similar weather patterns. Or the name of the region is given because of the approximate geographic location of the states within the country.

Show students the map of the Southeast region of the United States. Point out that the Southeast region includes the states of Arkansas, Louisiana, Mississippi, Alabama, Georgia, Florida, South Carolina, North Carolina, Tennessee, Kentucky, Virginia, West Virginia, Maryland, and Delaware. Show students where Washington, D.C., the capital of the United States, is located. Explain that Washington, D.C., lies between Maryland and Virginia.

Tell students to look at the small map of the United States. Point out the shaded Southeast region on the small map. Ask students why the fourteen states are called the Southeast region. Students may recognize that all the states are located in the southeast part of the United States.

Note that other regions of the United States are included in Weeks 19, 20, 21, and 25.

Introducing Vocabulary

border a line on a map showing the edge of a city, state, or country

capital a city where the government of a country or state is located

human-made feature a part of Earth such as a city or a road created by people

political map a map that shows human-made features

region a large area with common features

state a group of people united under one government; a state can be a whole country or part of a country, such as the United States

ANSWER KEY

Monday
1. 14
2. Any three of the following: Delaware, Florida, Georgia, Maryland, North Carolina, South Carolina, or Virginia

Tuesday
1. Alabama, Florida, Louisiana, and Mississippi
2. Arkansas and Louisiana

Wednesday
1. Washington, D.C.
2. between Virginia and Maryland

Thursday
1. Arkansas, Kentucky, Tennessee, and West Virginia
2. 4

Friday
1. Florida
2. Delaware and Maryland

Challenge
Students should label the nine capitals on the map.

Baton Rouge, Louisiana

Columbia, South Carolina

Jackson, Mississippi

Little Rock, Arkansas

Montgomery, Alabama

Nashville, Tennessee

Raleigh, North Carolina

Richmond, Virginia

Tallahassee, Florida

The Southeast Region of the United States

Washington, D.C., the capital of the United States, lies between Maryland and Virginia.

Map Key

★ state capital

✪ national capital

The Southeast Region of the United States

Monday

1. How many states are in the Southeast region? _____

2. Name three states that border the Atlantic Ocean.

    _____

Tuesday

1. Name the four states that border the Gulf of Mexico.

    _____

    _____

2. Name the two states that are farthest west.

    _____

Wednesday

1. What is the name of the capital of the United States?

    _____

2. Where is the capital of the United States located?

    _____

The Southeast Region of the United States

Thursday

1. Which four states do <u>not</u> border any labeled waterway?

   _____

2. How many states share a border with Alabama? _____

Friday

1. Which state is a large peninsula with small islands off its coast?

   _____

2. Which two states are located in the northeast tip of the Southeast region?

   _____

Challenge

Five state capitals are labeled on the map of the Southeast region. Nine are not labeled. Write the names of the nine capitals on the correct states. Use a United States map to help you with the names.

Capitals

Baton Rouge	Little Rock	Raleigh
Columbia	Montgomery	Richmond
Jackson	Nashville	Tallahassee

WEEK 23

Daily Geography

The Statue of Liberty

Introducing the Map

Tell students that places, buildings, structures, and statues have come to represent or symbolize a region. Give students the example of Mount Rushmore. When people think of Mount Rushmore, they think about the founding fathers of our country. Ask students to name some other cultural symbols in the United States. They may come up with such landmarks as the White House or the Lincoln Memorial.

Show students the map of New York City and the island on which the Statue of Liberty stands. Help students notice that the Statue of Liberty is on Liberty Island in New York Harbor. Read the labeled parts of the Statue of Liberty with students. Talk about how long ago people sailed to New York, and the first thing they saw was this statue. The Statue of Liberty welcomed new people to the country. She stood for liberty or freedom. This is true today as well. People immigrate to the U.S. from other countries. Many come through New York City, and they see this symbol of freedom. Millions of people also visit New York just to see this gigantic monument.

Share the following facts about the monument:

- The country of France gave the Statue of Liberty to the United States as a gift. The gift symbolizes the freedom and democracy that both countries share.

- The Statue of Liberty's complete name is "Liberty Enlightening the World." She is also called "Lady Liberty."

- The copper statue is 151 feet (46 meters) tall. She stands on a concrete and stone base that is 154 feet (47 meters) high. Around the statue's base is a star-shaped wall.

- Lady Liberty wears a flowing robe. On her head is a crown with seven spikes. She holds a burning torch in her right hand and a tablet in the other hand. A broken chain lies at her feet.

- You may wish to extend the lesson by adding more information about this famous landmark.

Introducing Vocabulary

cultural landmark a place selected and pointed out as important to a group of people

ferry a boat used to carry people across water

liberty freedom

monument a building or statue that honors people or events

state a group of people united under one government; a state can be a whole country or part of a country, such as the United States

ANSWER KEY

Monday
1. She is wearing a robe and a crown with seven spikes.
2. a torch and a tablet

Tuesday
1. Liberty Island
2. New York Harbor

Wednesday
1. 151 feet (46 meters) tall
2. 154 feet (47 meters) high

Thursday
1. New York City, New York
2. Lady Liberty or Liberty Enlightening the World

Friday
1. freedom
2. She welcomes people to America. She stands for freedom.

Challenge
Students should add a ferry to the New York Harbor.

The Statue of Liberty

The Statue of Liberty stands on Liberty Island in New York Harbor. The copper monument is 151 feet (46 meters) tall. She stands on a concrete and stone base. The base is 154 feet (47 meters) high. Lady Liberty welcomes people to America. She stands for liberty, which means FREEDOM!

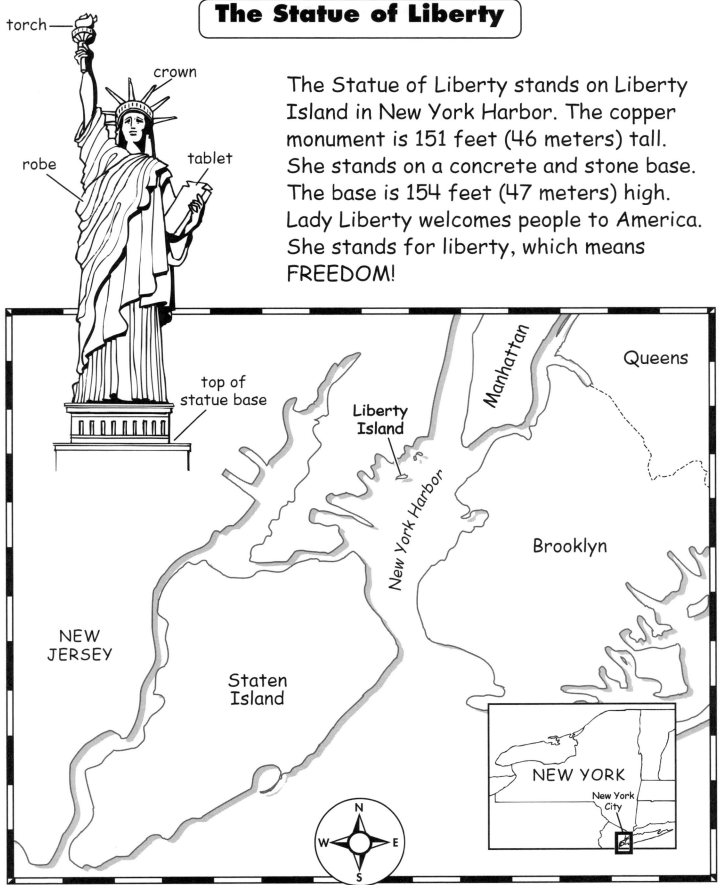

The Statue of Liberty

Monday

1. Describe what the Statue of Liberty is wearing.

_____

_____

2. Which two items is Lady Liberty holding?

_____

Tuesday

1. The Statue of Liberty stands on which island?

_____

2. The Statue of Liberty is located in which harbor?

_____

Wednesday

1. How tall is the Statue of Liberty?

_____

2. How tall is the base that the statue stands on?

_____

The Statue of Liberty

Thursday

1. In which city and state is the Statue of Liberty located?

   _____

2. What is another name for the Statue of Liberty?

   _____

Friday

1. Which word means the same as "liberty"—**freedom**, **joy**, or **friendship**?

   _____

2. Why is the Statue of Liberty important to the United States?

   _____

   _____

Challenge

To visit the Statue of Liberty, people take a ferry. On the map, draw a ferry going to the Statue of Liberty.

Daily Geography

The White House

Introducing the Map

Tell students that a cultural landmark is a place, building, structure, or statue that has come to represent or symbolize a region or culture. Give students the example of the Statue of Liberty. Ask students to name some other cultural landmarks in the United States. Most students will probably name monuments or buildings in Washington, D.C., such as the Washington Monument or the Lincoln Memorial.

Share with students that Washington, D.C., is the headquarters of the country's national government. The president, members of Congress, and thousands of other government employees work there. Ask students if they know where the White House is located. Explain that the address for the White House is 1600 Pennsylvania Avenue. The White House is a symbol for the country. It is a cultural landmark that stands for America's unity and democratic traditions.

Show students the grid map of the White House area in Washington, D.C. Name the buildings and Ellipse for students. Tell students the Ellipse is an oval-shaped, park-like area. Define other words for students such as *executive*, *reflecting*, and *department* as needed. Read the captions with students as well.

Share with students that this map has lines on it. These lines form a pattern called a grid. Tell students the definition of a grid. Expand on the definition by telling students that the squares formed by the grid are marked with letters and numbers. Point out the numbers and letters on the grid. Explain to students that grids on maps help people locate specific things on a map more readily.

Ask students to find the White House on the map. Explain that the White House is located in square A2. Check for understanding by having students find another building on the map. Practice using the grid squares to locate places on the map. Tell students that square A1 has been left blank. They will be adding something to that square on the challenge question.

Introducing Vocabulary

address the house number, street, city, state, and zip code where a person receives mail

cultural landmark a place selected and pointed out as important to a group of people

Ellipse an oval-shaped park in Washington, D.C.

grid a pattern of lines that form squares

monument a building or statue that honors people or events

ANSWER KEY

Monday
1. the president
2. 1600 Pennsylvania Avenue, Washington, D.C.

Tuesday
1. park
2. Department of the Treasury

Wednesday
1. an oval-shaped, park-like area; B2
2. Executive Office Building and the National Aquarium

Thursday
1. National Aquarium; B3
2. Museum of American History; C3

Friday
1. The Washington Monument honors George Washington. Some students may say the city is named after him, which is also true.
2. The view is of the Ellipse and the Washington Monument. Some students may name the Executive Office Building, the National Aquarium, the Reflecting Pool, and the Museum of American History.

Challenge
Answers will vary. Ideas might include an American flag, eagle, the Great Seal, or the Declaration of Independence. Guide students away from symbols that would not be found in Washington, D.C., such as the Statue of Liberty.

The White House

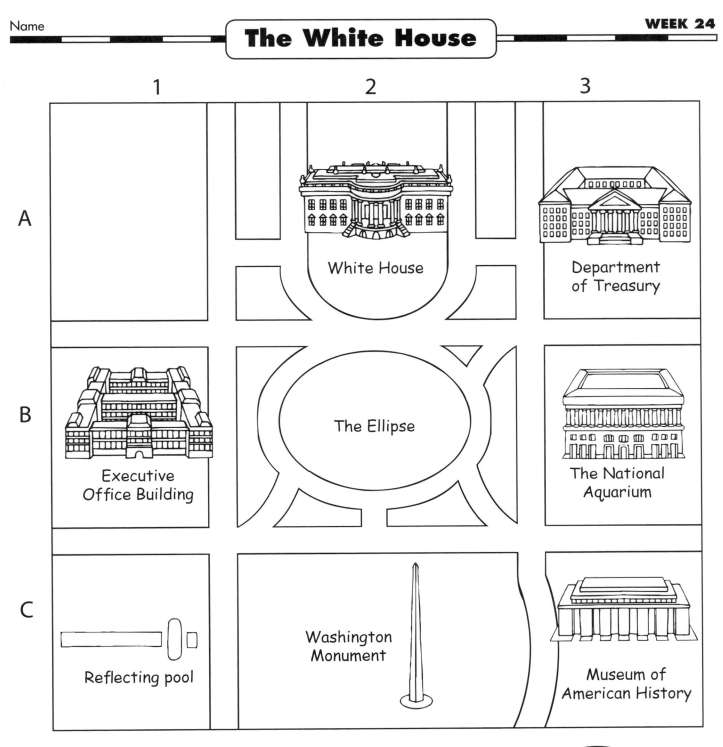

- The president of the United States lives and works in the White House.

- The White House is located at 1600 Pennsylvania Avenue, Washington, D.C.

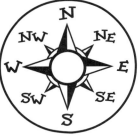

Name _____

The White House

Monday

1. Who lives and works in the White House?

_____

2. What is the address of the White House?

_____

Tuesday

1. Is there an office building or a park in front of the White House?

_____

2. Which building is next to the White House in square A3?

_____

Wednesday

1. What is the Ellipse? In which square is the Ellipse?

_____

2. Which two buildings are on either side of the Ellipse?

_____

_____

The White House

Thursday

1. Where would a tourist see different kinds of fish? In which square is that building?

   _____

2. Where would a tourist see displays of America's past? In which square is that building?

   _____

Friday

1. How is George Washington, the first president, honored in the nation's capital?

   _____

   _____

2. What could a person see from the front steps of the White House?

   _____

Challenge

In square A1 on the map, draw your favorite symbol of America. Remember, it should be found in Washington, D.C.

WEEK 25

Daily Geography

ANSWER KEY

Monday
1. 12
2. North-Central region

Tuesday
1. 60° and raining
2. 50° and partly cloudy

Wednesday
1. 45° and thunderstorms
2. Minnesota

Thursday
1. North Dakota; South Dakota
2. Kansas and Illinois

Friday
1. 6
2. Minnesota has the lowest temperature; Indiana has the highest temperature.

Challenge
Answers will vary. Students should pick a state and write about the weather and activities they could do. An example might be: "I would like to visit Minnesota, especially the northern part. Then I could see snow for the first time. I could go ice-skating or cross-country skiing. I could even build a snowman. It would be freezing cold, but a lot of fun."

A Weather Map

Introducing the Map

Introduce the term *weather*. Explain to students that weather is the condition of the air at a certain place and time. Tell students that there are many kinds of weather. The weather may be warm and sunny in one place and cold and raining in another. There are many ways to describe the weather. We talk about temperature, precipitation, and the sun. Explain to students that when you measure how hot or cold the air is, you are measuring the temperature of the air.

Explain that precipitation is any form of water that falls from clouds. Rain, snow, hail, and sleet are all different kinds of precipitation. Explain that sunlight carries energy, which warms up the Earth and affects our weather. Tell students that because air can flow, it carries heat from one place to another. This is what produces our weather.

Show students the weather map of the North-Central region of the United States. Talk about the states that make up this region. Point out the small map of the United States. Discuss the location of the region in the U.S. and what kinds of weather they think this area would have.

Look at the weather symbols used in the map key. Point out that the rain, snow, and thunderstorm symbols tell students that precipitation is taking place. The sun symbol tells students that the sun is shining. Explain that high temperatures indicate warm air flow and low temperatures indicate cool air flow.

Also, talk about how water freezes at 32°F. The Fahrenheit scale has been used for this lesson. You may wish to extend the lesson to include temperatures in degrees Celsius as well.

Introducing Vocabulary

degree a unit for measuring temperature (° is the symbol for degree)

precipitation rain, snow, sleet, hail, or drizzle

state a group of people united under one government; a state can be a whole country or part of a country, such as the United States

temperature a measure of how hot or cold the air is

weather the condition of the air at a certain place and time

The North-Central Region of the United States

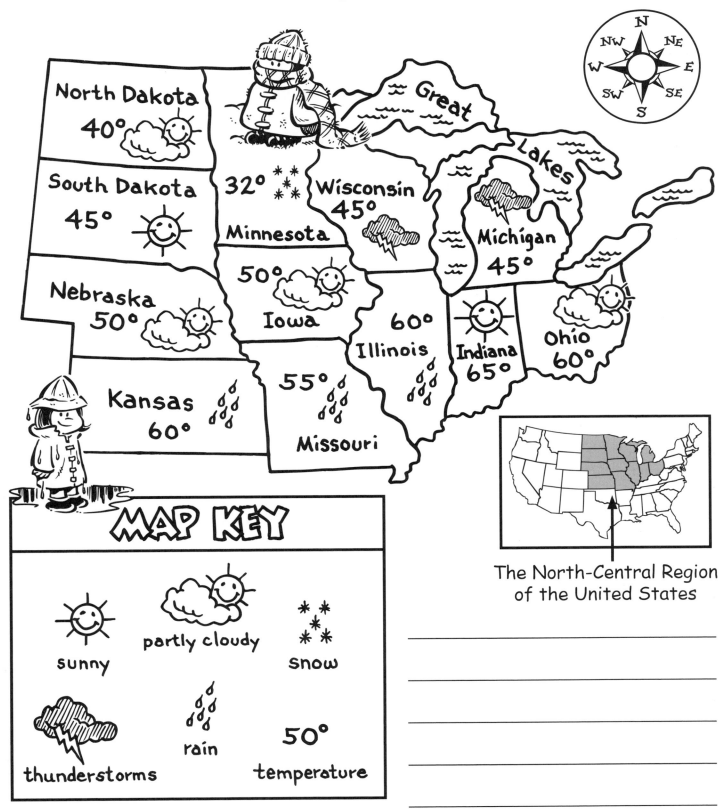

The North-Central Region of the United States

MAP KEY

sunny

partly cloudy

snow

thunderstorms

rain

50° temperature

A Weather Map

Monday

1. How many states are shown on the map?

_____

2. In which region of the United States are the states located?

_____

Tuesday

1. What is the weather like in Kansas?

_____

2. What is the weather like in Nebraska?

_____

Wednesday

1. What is the weather like in Wisconsin and Michigan?

_____

2. In which state is it snowing?

_____

Daily Geography

A Weather Map

WEEK 25

Thursday

1. Which state is 40° and partly cloudy? Which state is south of this state?

   _____

2. Which two states have temperatures of 60° and rain?

   _____

Friday

1. How many states border the Great Lakes?

   _____

2. Which state has the lowest temperature? Which state has the highest temperature?

   _____

Challenge

Choose which state in the North-Central region you would like to visit. On the map page, write about the weather in that state. Then write about the kinds of activities you could do in that kind of weather.

Skill: Ecosystems   Essential Element: 3: Standard 8

Oregon's Forests

Introducing the Map

Discuss with students that an ecosystem is a community of plants and animals, interacting with their environment. Talk about different ecosystems in the world such as grasslands and deserts. Another ecosystem that students will be familiar with is a forest. Tell students that a forest is a large area of land covered with trees. Explain that students will be looking at Oregon's forest ecosystem.

Show students the map of Oregon's forests. Give students background information on Oregon's forest ecosystem as they look at the map. Tell students that forests cover almost half of Oregon. The state is best known for its evergreen trees. Common names include cedar, fir, pine, and spruce trees. The state tree is the Douglas fir. Some of Oregon's Douglas firs reach heights of 250 feet (76 meters).

Share with students that Oregon has thirteen national forests. The forests are protected and preserved by the National Park Service. Tell students that forests are also planted in Oregon. Oregon produces more lumber than any other state. Oregon is also a major producer of Christmas trees that are shipped all over the country.

Read about the different plants and animals that are in the forests on the map page. Tell students that only a sampling of the many plants and animals of Oregon's forests are listed.

Introducing Vocabulary

ecosystem a community of plants and animals

forest a large area thickly covered with trees

national forest a forest managed and protected by the government

state a group of people united under one government; a state can be a whole country or part of a country, such as the United States

ANSWER KEY

Monday
1. forests
2. one-half of Oregon

Tuesday
1. Any three of the following: cedar, fir, pine, or spruce
2. Any three of the following: bear, beaver, deer, elk, fox, owl, or woodpecker

Wednesday
1. yes
2. Blue Mountains; yes

Thursday
1. Douglas fir
2. 13

Friday
1. Willamette River; forests and mountains
2. California, Idaho, and Washington; yes

Challenge
Students should color the trees on the map green. Students should choose a forest animal and draw it on the map.

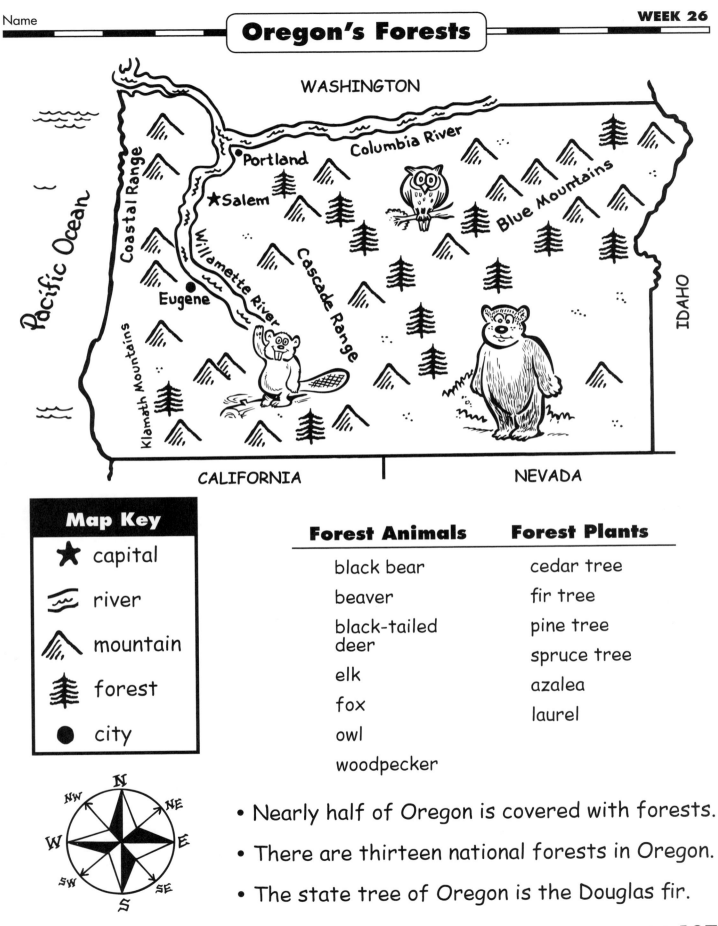

Map Key
- ★ capital
- river
- mountain
- forest
- ● city

Forest Animals
- black bear
- beaver
- black-tailed deer
- elk
- fox
- owl
- woodpecker

Forest Plants
- cedar tree
- fir tree
- pine tree
- spruce tree
- azalea
- laurel

- Nearly half of Oregon is covered with forests.

- There are thirteen national forests in Oregon.

- The state tree of Oregon is the Douglas fir.

Oregon's Forests

Monday

1. Oregon has many mountains and _____.

2. Do forests cover one-half or all of Oregon?

   _____

Tuesday

1. Name three kinds of trees that grow in Oregon.

   _____

2. Name three kinds of animals that live in the forest.

   _____

Wednesday

1. Are most of the forests near mountains in Oregon?

   _____

2. Which mountains are in northeast Oregon? Are there forests in this area, too?

   _____

   _____

Oregon's Forests

Thursday

1. What is the state tree of Oregon?

_____

2. How many national forests are in Oregon?

_____

Friday

1. Eugene, Portland, and Salem are all on which river? What kinds of landforms are near the three cities?

_____

_____

2. Which states border Oregon? Do you think those states have forests?

_____

Challenge

On the map, color the forests green. Choose an animal from the list and draw it on the map.

WEEK 27

Daily Geography

Ten Largest Cities in Wyoming

Introducing the Map

Introduce the term *population*. Explain to students that when you talk about the population of a city you are talking about the number of people who live in the city. Talk about how each state has a different total population. California has the largest population in the United States. It has several large cities like Los Angeles and San Diego. New York is another state that has a large population. New York City is the largest city in the U.S., with a population of over eight million people.

Discuss how some states are very large in area, but they have small populations. Show students the map and population chart of Wyoming. Explain that Wyoming is very large in area, but that it has the smallest population of all the states in the United States.

Show students the map of the state of Wyoming. Have students look at the cities on the map and read their populations from the chart. Ask students which city on the map has the largest population. Cheyenne, the capital, has the largest population. Have students point to its location on the map. Check for understanding by repeating this process with another city on the map. Help students notice that all the cities, except Cheyenne, have fewer than 50,000 people.

In this lesson, students will practice reading a map and a chart. You may wish to extend the lesson to include a discussion about the census. Tell students that the census is taken every ten years in the United States.

ANSWER KEY

Monday
1. The map shows the state of Wyoming with the 10 largest cities labeled. It also shows the rivers.
2. The chart shows the names of the cities and their populations.

Tuesday
1. Cheyenne
2. largest city

Wednesday
1. Sheridan; north
2. Green River; 11,808 people

Thursday
1. less than 12,000
2. Riverton; Bighorn River

Friday
1. Casper; North Platte River
2. Cody and Riverton; Bighorn River

Challenge
Students should number the three largest cities on the map as follows:
1. Cheyenne
2. Casper
3. Laramie

Introducing Vocabulary

capital a city where the government of a country or state is located

city a very large or important town

population the total number of people who live in a place

state a group of people united under one government; a state can be a whole country or part of a country, such as the United States

Ten Largest Cities in Wyoming

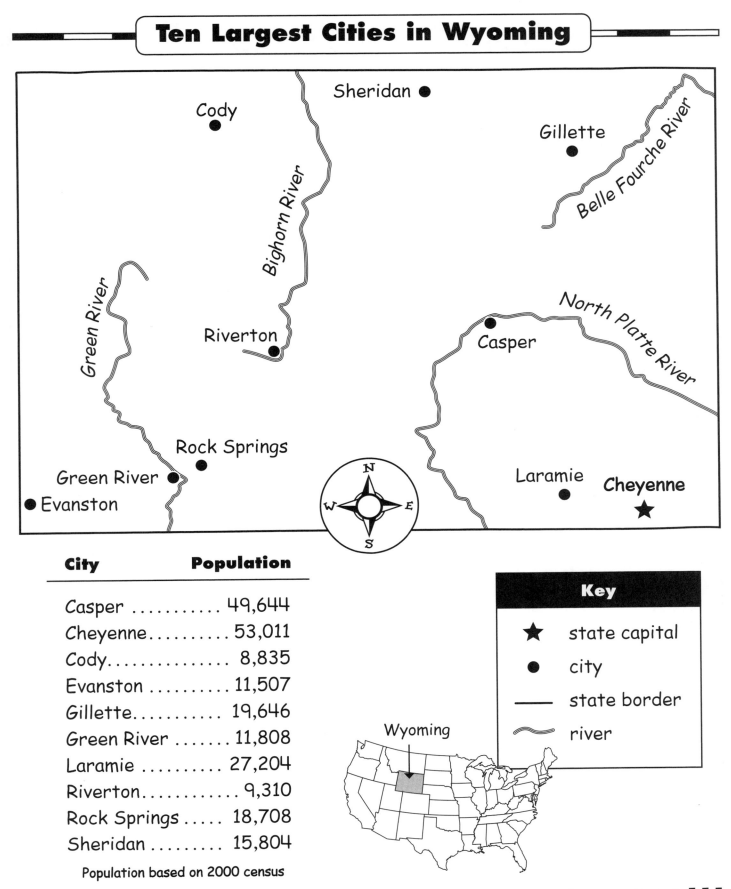

City	Population
Casper	49,644
Cheyenne	53,011
Cody	8,835
Evanston	11,507
Gillette	19,646
Green River	11,808
Laramie	27,204
Riverton	9,310
Rock Springs	18,708
Sheridan	15,804

Population based on 2000 census

Key

★ state capital

● city

— state border

〰 river

Wyoming

Ten Largest Cities in Wyoming

Monday

1. What does the map show?

   _____

   _____

2. What does the chart show?

   _____

Tuesday

1. What is the capital of Wyoming?

   _____

2. Is the capital the largest or smallest city?

   _____

Wednesday

1. Which city has a population of 15,804? Is it north or south of the capital?

   _____

2. Which city and river have the same name? What is the city's population?

   _____

Daily Geography

Ten Largest Cities in Wyoming

Thursday

1. Is Evanston's population more or less than 12,000?

   _____

2. Which city has a population of 9,310? Which river is it on?

   _____

Friday

1. Which city is the second largest in population? Which river is it on?

   _____

   _____

2. Which two cities have the smallest populations?

   _____

Challenge

On the map, number the three largest cities from largest to smallest in population. For example, Cheyenne is #1.

A County Fair

Introducing the Map

Explain to students that the term *culture* is used to explain a way of life. Culture includes ideas, art, customs, and traditions. A custom can be a tradition that is passed down through many generations. One example of a custom would be a town that celebrates Independence Day with a parade each year. Ask students for other examples of customs they have in their families.

One custom many communities have is a county fair. Students may remember the county fair in the book *Charlotte's Web,* or they may have attended or participated in the county fair in their area. Discuss things they have experienced at the county fair.

Explain that a county fair may include animals, shows, rides, games, and food. Tell students that people from the community often enter their handmade goods such as art, crafts, and baked goods into a contest at the county fair. People show the animals or livestock they have raised. The animals are judged and receive ribbons for things like "best of show." Carnivals and grandstand acts are also parts of a typical county fair.

Show students the county fair map. Talk about the different areas and what kinds of things are located in each area. Be sure to read the labels on the map and review the vocabulary words with students.

Introducing Vocabulary

carnival a fair or festival with rides and games

county a part of a state; states are divided into counties

culture a way of life, ideas, customs, and traditions

custom a way of acting; something that is done regularly

exhibit a public show

fair a public show of farm products and animals, often with entertainment, games, and rides

livestock animals raised on a farm or ranch

ANSWER KEY

Monday
1. A County Fair
2. Any three of the following areas: carnival, food, games, gate, grandstand, livestock or animal area, and restrooms

Tuesday
1. carnival
2. balloon dart and duck toss

Wednesday
1. Any three of the following: chickens, cows, hogs, horses, rabbits, or sheep
2. birdhouse, paintings, and rugs

Thursday
1. Juggling Brothers
2. Snack Shack

Friday
1. Ferris wheel and the airplane ride
2. roller coaster

Challenge
Students should write about their favorite part of the county fair and give reasons why it is their favorite.

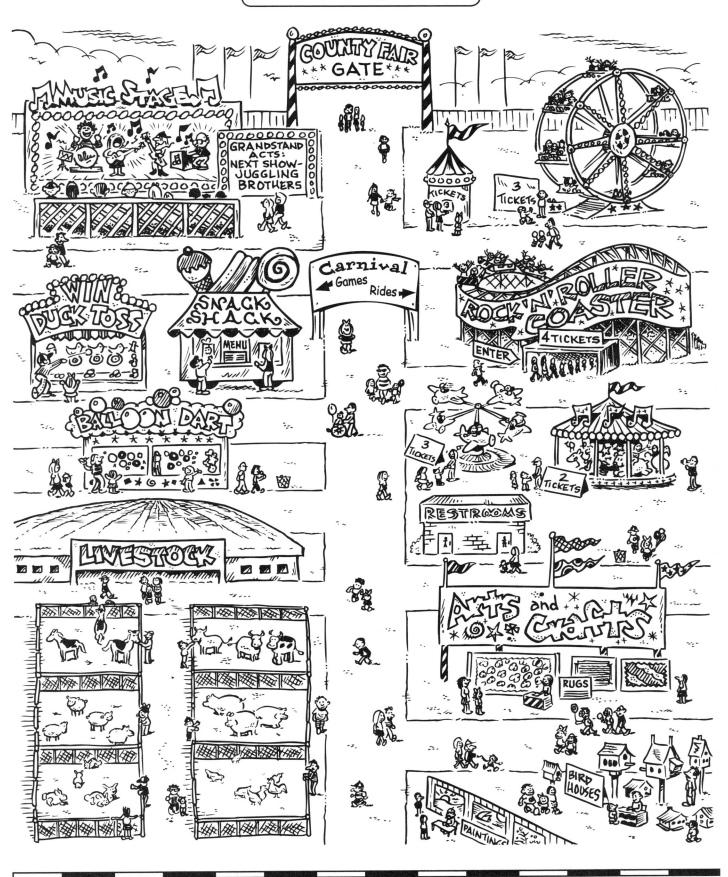

Daily Geography

A County Fair

Monday

1. What is the title of the map?

_____

2. Name three areas at the county fair.

_____

Tuesday

1. Name the area that has fun rides.

_____

2. Which games are in the game area?

_____

Wednesday

1. Name three kinds of animals that are at the county fair.

_____

2. What things have people made to show at the fair?

_____

A County Fair

Thursday

1. Who is performing next at the Grandstand?

   _____

2. Where can you eat at the fair?

   _____

Friday

1. Which rides cost 3 tickets?

   _____

2. Which ride costs the most tickets?

   _____

Challenge

Which part at the county fair is your favorite? On the back of the map, write about your favorite part of the county fair and tell why you like it.

WEEK 29

Daily Geography

ANSWER KEY

Monday
1. 15
2. cheese and butter

Tuesday
1. east of the Wisconsin River
2. 16,623 dairy farms

Wednesday
1. 76 dairy cows
2. 2,019 gallons of milk

Thursday
1. America's Dairyland
2. Green Bay, Madison, and Milwaukee; Green Bay

Friday
1. 20 pounds of milk makes 2 pounds of cheese
2. 42 pounds of milk makes 2 pounds of butter

Challenge
Students should draw a milk carton, a block of cheese, and a stick of butter near the facts on the map page.

A Product Map: Wisconsin

Introducing the Map

Tell students that many states produce or make the food we buy in stores. Sometimes a state is known for the product that it grows or makes. For example, Florida is known for the oranges it grows. Idaho is known for its potatoes. Iowa is famous for the production of corn and hogs.

Show students the product map of Wisconsin. Point out the symbols in the map key and on the map. Explain to students that the cow icon represents areas where dairy farms are located in the state, not the location of individual farms. Discuss the different areas of the state that have dairy farms. Help students notice that the eastern part of the state has the most dairy farms. Talk about the cities that are located in this area as well. Mention that there are a few areas west of the Wisconsin River that have dairy farms, but that the northern part of the state is not known for dairy farming. Tell students the northern part of Wisconsin is made up mostly of forests.

Share with students that Wisconsin is known as "America's Dairyland" because it is the top producer of milk and milk products. The milk is used to make different kinds of cheese and butter. Read other interesting facts about dairy farming on the map with students. The dairy statistics are from the Wisconsin Agricultural Statistics Service (WASS), May 2003.

Introducing Vocabulary

dairy farm a farm where cows are raised for their milk

product something that is made by a natural process like corn, dairy cows, or minerals

product map a map that shows products such as corn, dairy cows, or minerals

state a group of people united under one government; a state can be a whole country or part of a country, such as the United States

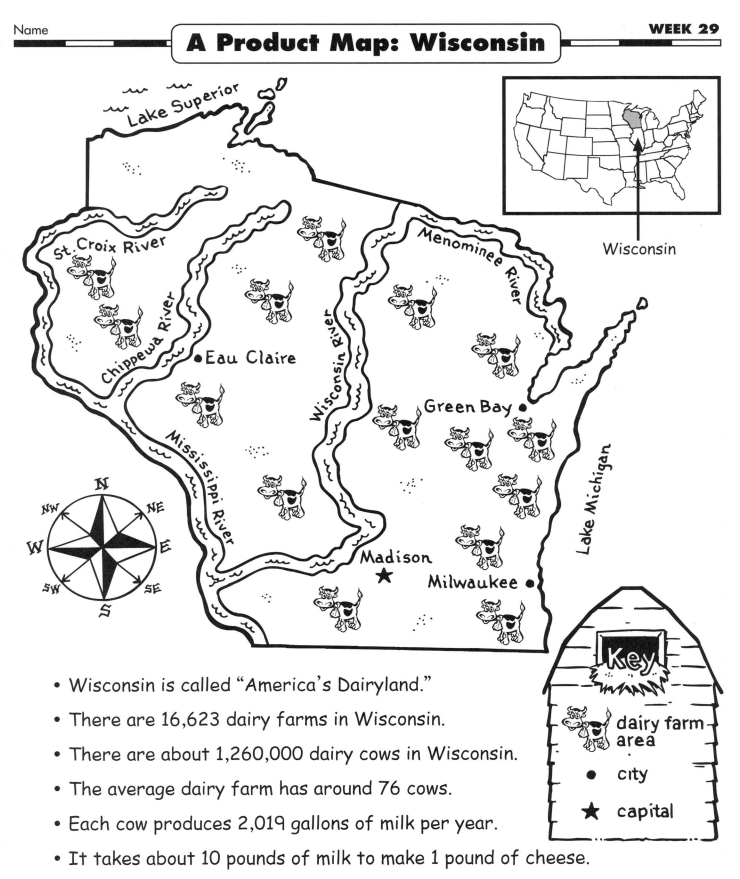

- Wisconsin is called "America's Dairyland."

- There are 16,623 dairy farms in Wisconsin.

- There are about 1,260,000 dairy cows in Wisconsin.

- The average dairy farm has around 76 cows.

- Each cow produces 2,019 gallons of milk per year.

- It takes about 10 pounds of milk to make 1 pound of cheese.

- It takes about 21 pounds of milk to make 1 pound of butter.

A Product Map: Wisconsin

Monday

1. How many areas of Wisconsin have dairy farms?

   _____

2. Name two dairy products made from milk.

   _____

Tuesday

1. Are most of the dairy farm areas east or west of the Wisconsin River?

   _____

2. How many dairy farms are in Wisconsin?

   _____

Wednesday

1. Each dairy farm has about how many dairy cows?

   _____

2. How much milk does a dairy cow produce in one year?

   _____

A Product Map: Wisconsin

Thursday

1. What is Wisconsin's nickname?

   _____

2. Which three cities are east of the Wisconsin River? Which city has more dairy farms near it?

   _____

   _____

Friday

1. _____ pounds of milk make 2 pounds of cheese.

2. _____ pounds of milk make 2 pounds of butter.

Challenge

The three main dairy products are milk, cheese, and butter. Draw a milk carton, a block of cheese, and a stick of butter near the facts on the map.

Living in a Community

Introducing the Map

Ask students to name different kinds of homes people live in. They will probably name such places as houses, apartments, duplexes, and mobile homes. Talk about how every community is made up of different types of homes to live in. Ask students if there are different types of homes in their neighborhood. Discuss the differences between a house, a duplex, apartments, and a mobile home.

Show students the map of the fictitious community. Share with students that this community is a good example of a community that has different types of homes.

Look at the map to find an example of each type of home. Have students look at the addresses on the homes. Point out that each home has a different address. Explain to students that they can figure out the street address by looking at which street the entrance is on. For example, the Tower Apartments are on Green Avenue, and the Mobile Home Park is on First Street. Tell students that an address includes numbers and a street name. For example, 1240 Dirk Street. Explain to students that a complete address also includes a city, state, and zip code.

Introducing Vocabulary

address the house number, street, city, state, and zip code where a person usually receives mail

apartment a set of rooms to live in, usually on one floor of a building

community a group of people who live together in the same area

duplex two houses that are attached by a wall

house a building where people live

mobile home a large trailer that people live in

WEEK 30

Daily Geography

ANSWER KEY

Monday
1. four
2. Green Avenue

Tuesday
1. Tower Apartments
2. 4310 Green Avenue

Wednesday
1. First Street
2. 96, 97, and 98 First Street

Thursday
1. mobile homes
2. duplexes

Friday
1. Brown Avenue
2. 11, 12, 13 Green Avenue

Challenge
Answers will vary. Students should write about which kind of home they like and why. An example might be: "I would like to live in a tall apartment building. That way, family and friends could live near me in the same building."

Living in a Community

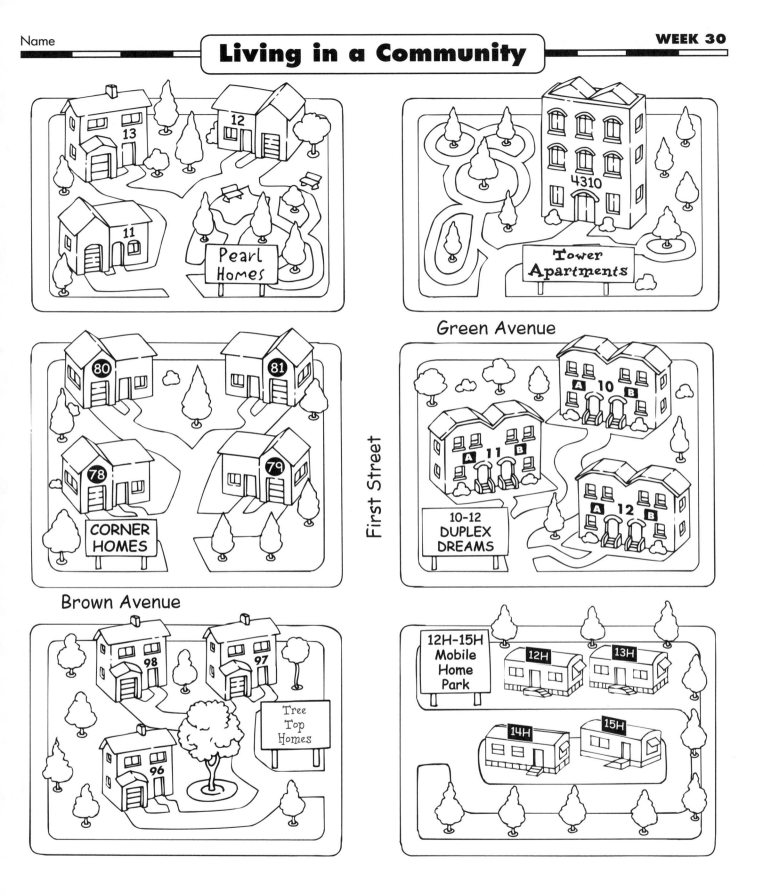

Living in a Community

Monday

1. How many different types of homes are shown on this map?

   _____

2. On which street are the Pearl Homes located?

   _____

Tuesday

1. What is the name of the apartment building on Green Avenue?

   _____

2. What is the address of the apartment building?

   _____

Wednesday

1. On which street are the Tree Top Homes?

   _____

2. What are the addresses for the Tree Top Homes?

   _____

Living in a Community

Thursday

1. Which type of homes are located at 12 H–15 H First Street?

   _____

2. Which type of homes are located at 10–12 Brown Avenue?

   _____

Friday

1. On which street are the Corner Homes located?

   _____

2. What are the addresses of the Pearl Homes?

   _____

Challenge

Which kind of house would you like to live in? On the map, write about your favorite kind of house and tell why you like it.

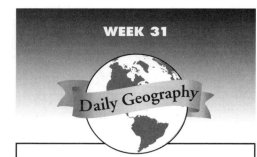

Daily Geography

ANSWER KEY

Monday
1. services
2. School, Fire Station, Courthouse

Tuesday
1. Post Office, Police Station, Water Company
2. 1000 Express Street

Wednesday
1. 500 Care Street
2. Express Street

Thursday
1. Care Street
2. Safety Street

Friday
1. the bus service
2. 10

Challenge
Students should color the police station, the hospital, and the fire station.

Community Services

Introducing the Map

Explain to students that businesses and people in a community work together to take care of the people in a community. Communities are provided with services. Some services in a community include the police station, fire station, hospitals, post office, schools, library, courthouse, bus services, and the water company. Ask students if they have these services in their community. Talk about the different locations of the services in your community.

Show students the map of the fictitious community. Share with students that this map shows different types of community services. Discuss the emergency community services shown on the map. Have students look at the addresses on the buildings. Point out that each building has a different address. Explain to students that they can figure out the street address by looking at which street the entrance is on. For example, the Library is located on 300 Care Street.

Not all the community services in a community are on this map. You may wish to extend the lesson to discuss others that may be included.

Introducing Vocabulary

address the house number, street, city, state, and zip code where a person usually receives mail

community a group of people who live together in the same area

community services public places that provide for the needs of a community such as: schools, hospitals, police stations, and parks

Community Services

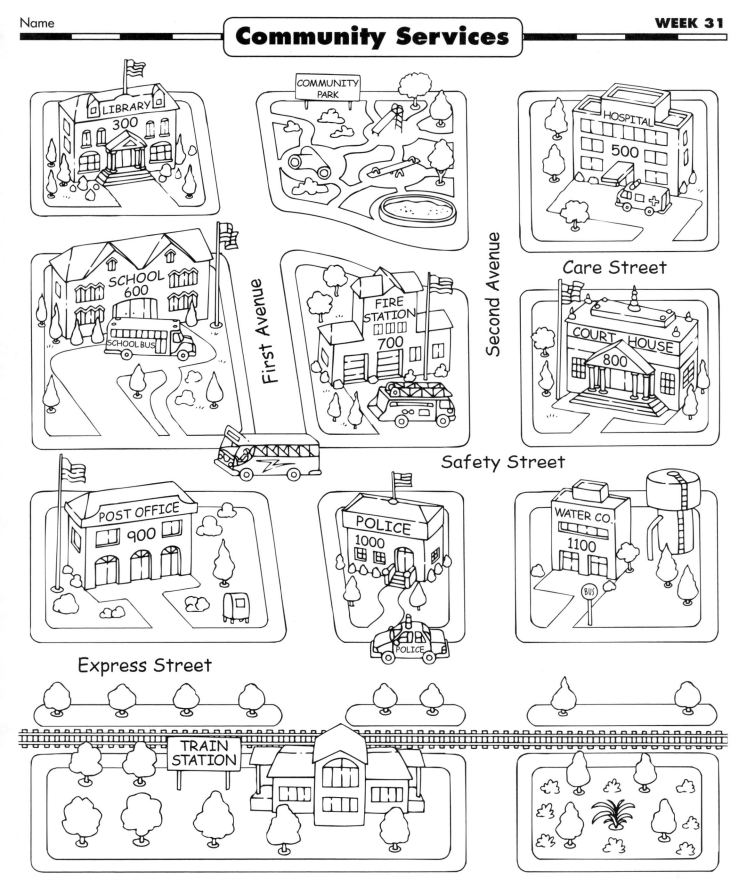

A community provides services for its people.

Community Services

Monday

1. A community provides _____ for its people.

2. Which community services have entrances on Safety Street?

   _____

   _____

Tuesday

1. Which community services are located on Express Street?

   _____

   _____

2. What is the address of the police station?

   _____

Wednesday

1. What is the address of the hospital?

   _____

2. On which street can you mail a letter?

   _____

Community Services

Thursday

1. The park is a community service also. On which street is the park located?

   _____

2. The courthouse is located on the corner of Second Avenue and

   _____ .

Friday

1. Which community service helps you get around town?

   _____

2. How many community services are shown on this map?

   _____

Challenge

Color the community services on the map that handle emergencies.

ANSWER KEY

Monday
1. Bluegrass Region
2. northeast part of the state

Tuesday
1. Kentucky and Ohio Rivers
2. Appalachian Mountains

Wednesday
1. Frankfort; Kentucky River
2. Frankfort and Lexington

Thursday
1. They are champion thoroughbred horses.
2. a horse race called the Kentucky Derby

Friday
1. spring
2. Cumberland, Green, and Mississippi Rivers

Challenge
Students should color the Bluegrass Region blue-green.

Skill: Land Use   Essential Element 5: Standard 14

The Bluegrass Region of Kentucky

Introducing the Map

Explain to students that humans depend on the land for many needs. Humans have changed the land around them for such uses as houses, growing crops, and finding natural resources such as coal and oil.

Tell students that different communities use land in different ways. Some communities grow fruits and vegetables on the land; some communities raise animals on the land; and some communities have large National Parks on the land. The way people use land shapes the culture of the people.

Explain to students that the state of Kentucky has different types of land. It has large fields of farmland, rolling hills, several rivers, forests, mountains, and caves. Kentucky's different land areas are called regions. Show students the map of the Bluegrass Region of Kentucky. Talk about how this region is good for raising livestock. This region has a special kind of grass. Bluegrass is really green, but blue buds in the spring make the grass appear a bluish-green color. Read the facts about the region with students.

Tell students that champion racehorses are raised in the Bluegrass Region. Point out Lexington, Kentucky, on the map. Tell students that Lexington, Kentucky, is known as the "horse capital of the world." Explain to students that much of the land in Lexington is used for horse farms. A famous horse race called the "Kentucky Derby" is held in Louisville, Kentucky. Point out other physical features such as rivers and mountains in Kentucky.

Introducing Vocabulary

bluegrass a grass that has tiny bluish-green buds

livestock animals raised on a farm or ranch

mountain a piece of land that has steep sides and a round or pointed peak; higher than a hill

physical feature a natural part of Earth such as a mountain or an ocean

region a large area with common features

river a large stream that flows into a larger river, lake, sea, or ocean

state a group of people united under one government; a state can be a whole country or part of a country, such as the United States

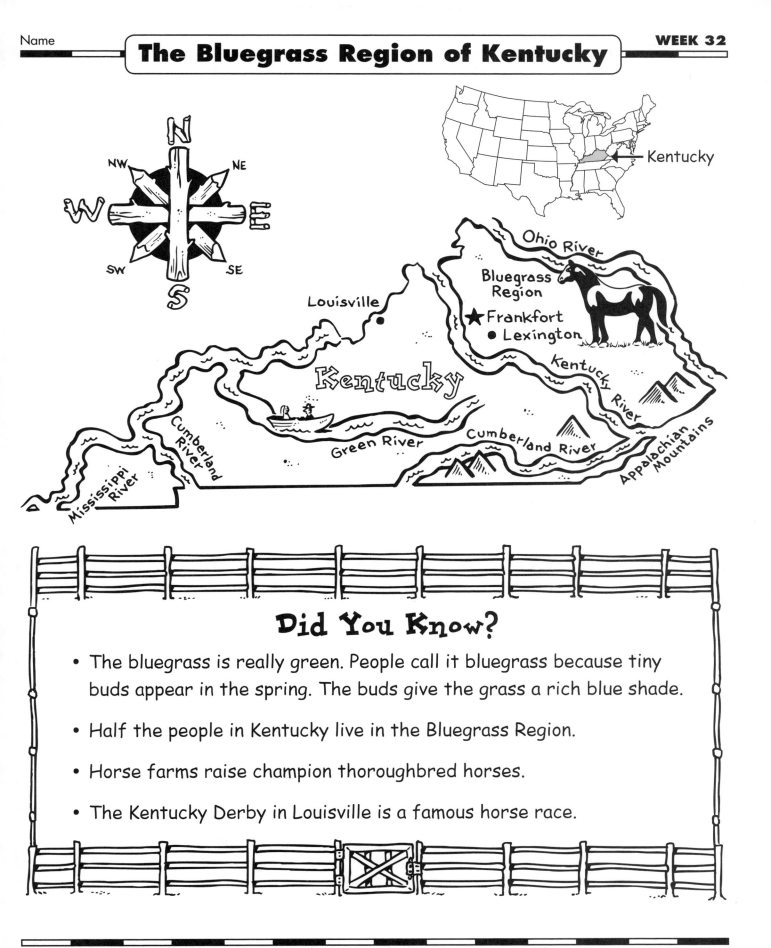

Kentucky

Did You Know?

• The bluegrass is really green. People call it bluegrass because tiny buds appear in the spring. The buds give the grass a rich blue shade.

• Half the people in Kentucky live in the Bluegrass Region.

• Horse farms raise champion thoroughbred horses.

• The Kentucky Derby in Louisville is a famous horse race.

The Bluegrass Region of Kentucky

Monday

1. Which region in Kentucky has many horse farms?

   _____

2. In which part of the state is this region?

   _____

Tuesday

1. Which two rivers border the Bluegrass Region?

   _____

2. Which mountains are southeast of the Bluegrass Region?

   _____

Wednesday

1. What is the capital of Kentucky? On which river is it located?

   _____

2. Which cities on the map are located in the Bluegrass Region?

   _____

The Bluegrass Region of Kentucky

Thursday

1. What is special about the horses in the Bluegrass Region?

   _____

   _____

2. What special event happens in Louisville every year?

   _____

Friday

1. Which season of the year does the grass look more blue-green?

   _____

2. Which rivers in Kentucky are <u>not</u> located in the Bluegrass Region?

   _____

   _____

Challenge

Lexington is called the "horse capital of the world." On the map, color the Bluegrass Region blue-green.

A Tourist Map: California

Introducing the Map

Ask students to name a state they would like to visit and tell why. An example might be the state of New York. Students may point out cities they would like to visit such as New York City or Buffalo. Physical features might include such places as Niagara Falls or Long Island. Human-made features might include the Statue of Liberty or Radio City Music Hall.

Explain to students that the physical features of a state help to determine what kinds of tourist attractions are possible. Show students the tourist map of California. Discuss the physical features of the state. Point out that many tourists come to California to see the Pacific Ocean. They come to go whale watching or visit the islands along the coast. They also come to hike in the mountains or see giant redwood trees. Point out famous landmarks such as Lassen Volcano, Lake Tahoe, and the Mojave Desert. Students should notice the national parks that are featured as well.

Talk about other human-made tourist attractions on the map such as Disneyland, Golden Gate Bridge, Hollywood, and the Monterey Bay Aquarium.

Remind students that only a sampling of the tourist attractions in California are on the map. You may wish to extend the lesson by adding more attractions to the map.

Introducing Vocabulary

coast land that is next to an ocean or sea

human-made feature a part of Earth such as a city or a road created by people

physical feature a natural part of Earth such as a mountain or an ocean

state a group of people united under one government; a state can be a whole country or part of a country, such as the United States

tourist a person who travels on a vacation

tourist map a map that shows interesting places for people to see

ANSWER KEY

Monday
1. California
2. Pacific Ocean

Tuesday
1. Any two of the following: Channel Islands, Disneyland, Hollywood, Mojave Desert, and San Diego Zoo. The cities of Anaheim, Los Angeles, or San Diego could also be considered tourist places. The Pacific Ocean is also a tourist attraction.
2. Any two of the following: Lake Tahoe, Lassen Volcano, and Redwood National Forest. The capital of Sacramento could also be considered a tourist place. The Pacific Ocean is also a tourist attraction.

Wednesday
1. Monterey Bay Aquarium
2. Any two of the following: boating or sailing, deep-sea diving, fishing, sailing, snorkeling, swimming, and surfing

Thursday
1. San Francisco; coast
2. Channel Islands

Friday
1. San Diego; southern California
2. Disneyland; Los Angeles and San Diego

Challenge
Students should add the Coast Ranges and Sierra Nevada to the map. The Coast Ranges are along the west coast of the state, and the Sierra Nevada are along the eastern border of the state.

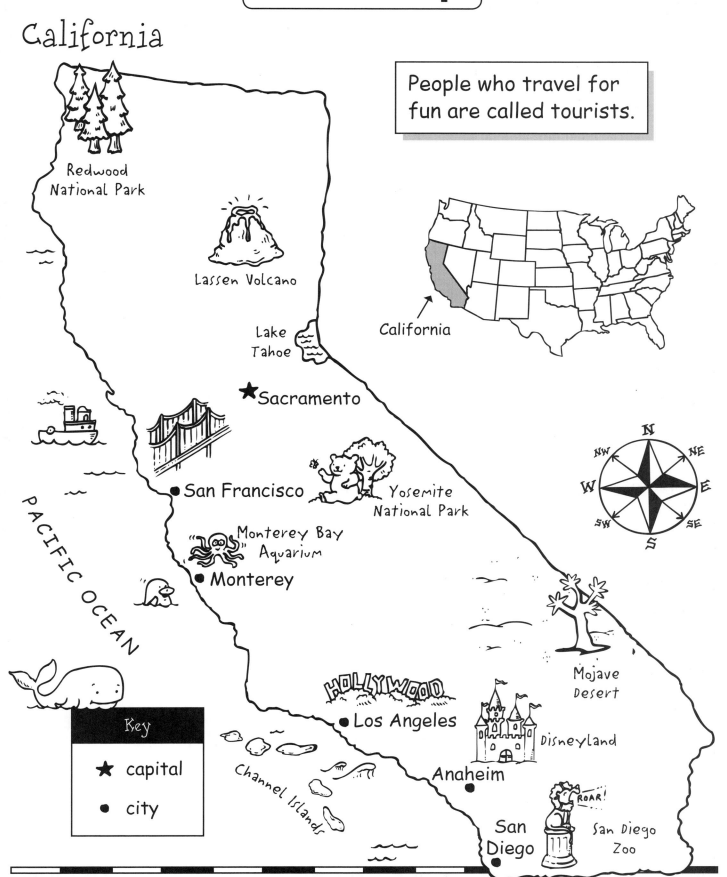

California

People who travel for fun are called tourists.

A Tourist Map: California

Monday

1. Which state is shown on the map?

   _____

2. Which ocean is shown on the map?

   _____

Tuesday

1. Name two tourist attractions south of San Francisco.

   _____

2. Name two tourist attractions north of San Francisco.

   _____

Wednesday

1. Which tourist attraction is in Monterey?

   _____

2. Name two things tourists could do in the Pacific Ocean.

   _____

A Tourist Map: California

Thursday

1. In which city is the Golden Gate Bridge located? Is the city on the coast or inland?

_____

2. Which islands are located off the coast of California?

_____

Friday

1. There is a famous zoo in which city? Is the city in the southern, central, or northern part of the state?

_____

2. Which famous tourist attraction is located in Anaheim? Which cities are near Anaheim?

_____

_____

Challenge

California has beautiful mountains. The Coast Ranges are up and down the west coast of California. The Sierra Nevada Range is between Lake Tahoe and the Mohave Desert. Draw mountains in those two areas. Add the names of the mountains to the map.

WEEK 34

Daily Geography

Minerals of Alaska

Introducing the Map

Ask students to name a natural resource. Students may say resources such as air, water, and land. Tell students that natural resources include those things, but that there are also mineral natural resources on Earth.

Mineral resources include coal, oil, stone, and sand. Fossil fuels—coal, oil, and natural gas—provide heat, light, and power to many people. Explain that mineral fuels or fossil fuels can be used up. They are limited.

Show students the map of Alaska. Talk about the following fuels that are mined in Alaska: oil and natural gas. Read the map key with the students and have them locate the different minerals shown on the map. Share with students that Alaska produces almost two million barrels of oil per day. It produces 25% of the oil in the United States. Alaska produces 1.25 billion cubic feet of natural gas a day. To put it simply, tell students that's a lot of natural gas! Please note that these statistics may change from year to year.

Talk about another important mineral in Alaska–the metal gold. Tell students that Alaska has rich deposits of gold near Fairbanks and Nome. Read the "Did You Know" facts with students.

Introducing Vocabulary

fossil fuels natural gas, oil, and coal

mineral something found in nature like gold or silver

mining taking rocks and minerals out of the Earth

natural resources materials supplied by nature that are useful or necessary for life such as forests, water, and minerals

state a group of people united under one government; a state can be a whole country or part of a country, such as the United States

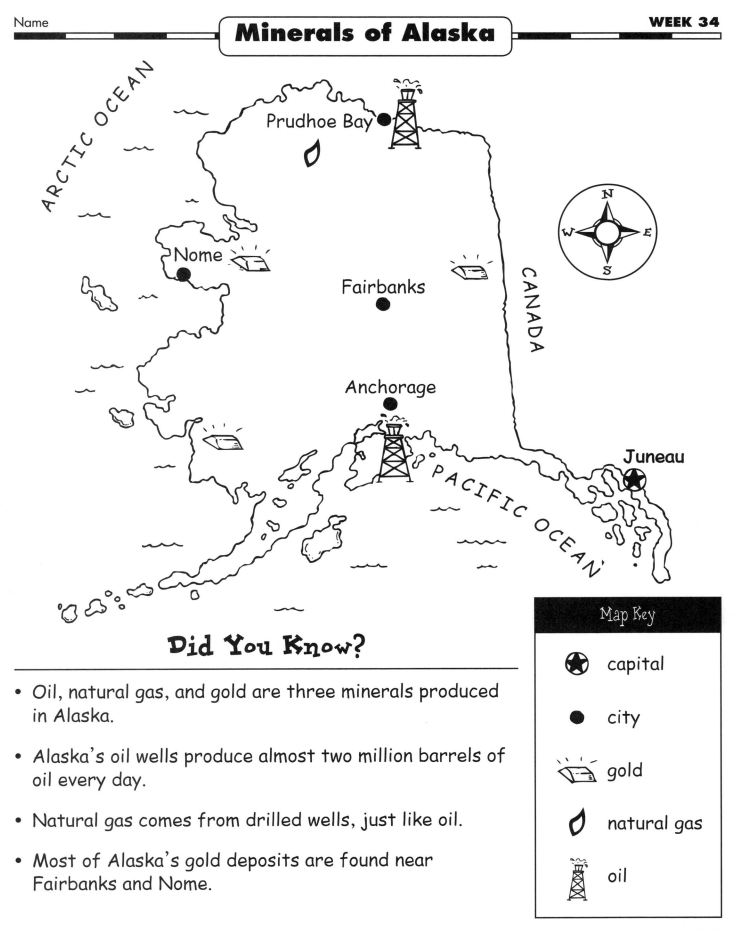

Did You Know?

• Oil, natural gas, and gold are three minerals produced in Alaska.

• Alaska's oil wells produce almost two million barrels of oil every day.

• Natural gas comes from drilled wells, just like oil.

• Most of Alaska's gold deposits are found near Fairbanks and Nome.

Map Key

⭐ capital

● city

gold

natural gas

oil

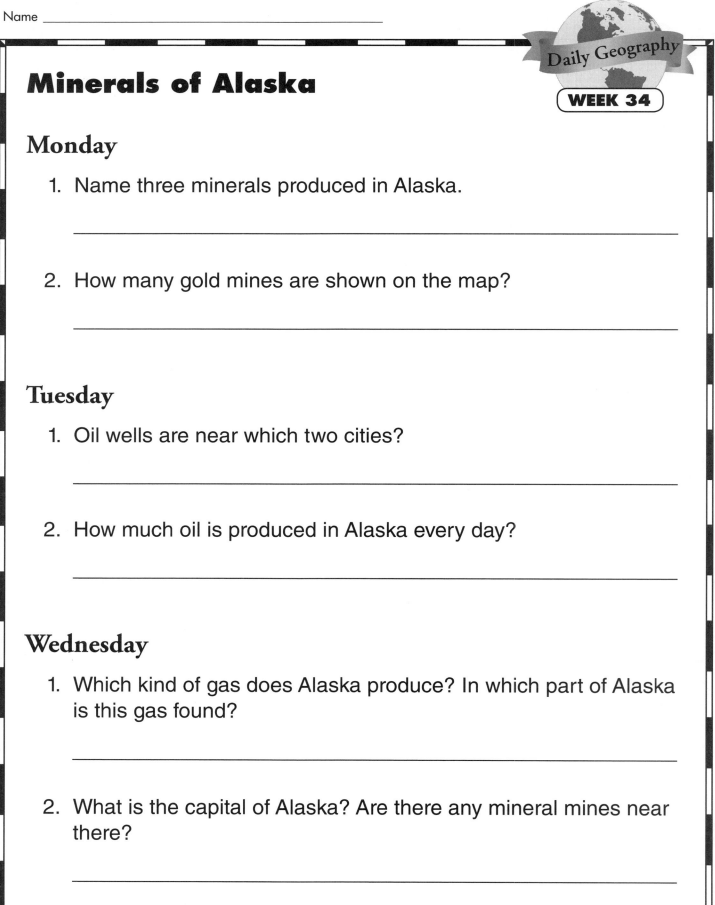

Minerals of Alaska

Monday

1. Name three minerals produced in Alaska.

   _____

2. How many gold mines are shown on the map?

   _____

Tuesday

1. Oil wells are near which two cities?

   _____

2. How much oil is produced in Alaska every day?

   _____

Wednesday

1. Which kind of gas does Alaska produce? In which part of Alaska is this gas found?

   _____

2. What is the capital of Alaska? Are there any mineral mines near there?

   _____

Minerals of Alaska

Thursday

1. Which area of Alaska mines for all three minerals?

   _____

2. Which country borders Alaska? Which mineral is located along this border?

   _____

Friday

1. Sometimes oil is drilled offshore in the ocean. Which oceans border Alaska?

   _____

2. Most of the gold deposits in Alaska are near which two cities?

   _____

Challenge

Color all the minerals on the map.

Daily Geography

The Lewis and Clark Trail

Introducing the Map

Ask students if they have ever looked at maps that show what places were like long ago. An example might include a map of a colonial town. Tell students that this kind of map would be called a history map.

Show students the map of The Lewis and Clark Trail. Share with students that this map shows a time when the eastern part of the United States was divided into states and territories, while the West was wilderness. Explain that Thomas Jefferson, the third president of the United States, purchased new lands, called the Louisiana Territory, from France in 1803.

This purchase doubled the size of the United States. President Jefferson wanted to expand the United States by exploring the new territory. He also wanted to find an easy route to the Pacific Ocean.

President Jefferson decided to send his secretary Meriwether Lewis and former army commander William Clark to explore the new territory. On May 14, 1804, Lewis, Clark, and about 40 other men began the long journey that would take them more than 8,000 miles (12,800 km) from St. Louis to the Pacific Ocean and back. Lewis and Clark made maps and kept journals along the way. People used the maps and journals to open up the western wilderness to new settlers.

Have students follow the trail from St. Louis, Missouri, to the Pacific Ocean. Read the caption and look at the pictures of the two explorers. Review the vocabulary with students.

Introducing Vocabulary

explore to travel in order to discover new things

history map a map that shows places or events from long ago

route a way to go from one place to another

territory any large area of land

trail a path

wilderness a natural place that is undisturbed by humans

ANSWER KEY

Monday
1. an explorer
2. Lewis and Clark

Tuesday
1. St. Louis
2. the Pacific Ocean

Wednesday
1. wilderness
2. the Missouri River

Thursday
1. 8,000 miles
2. 1804; 1806

Friday
1. new lands for the U.S.
2. People settled the lands and the area became part of the U.S.

Challenge
Answers will vary. An example of a journal entry might be: "Today I saw herds of buffalo. I also saw lots of deer. There was a bear drinking from the river. I stayed away from him. Tomorrow we will stay near the Missouri River as we head farther west."

Name

The Lewis and Clark Trail

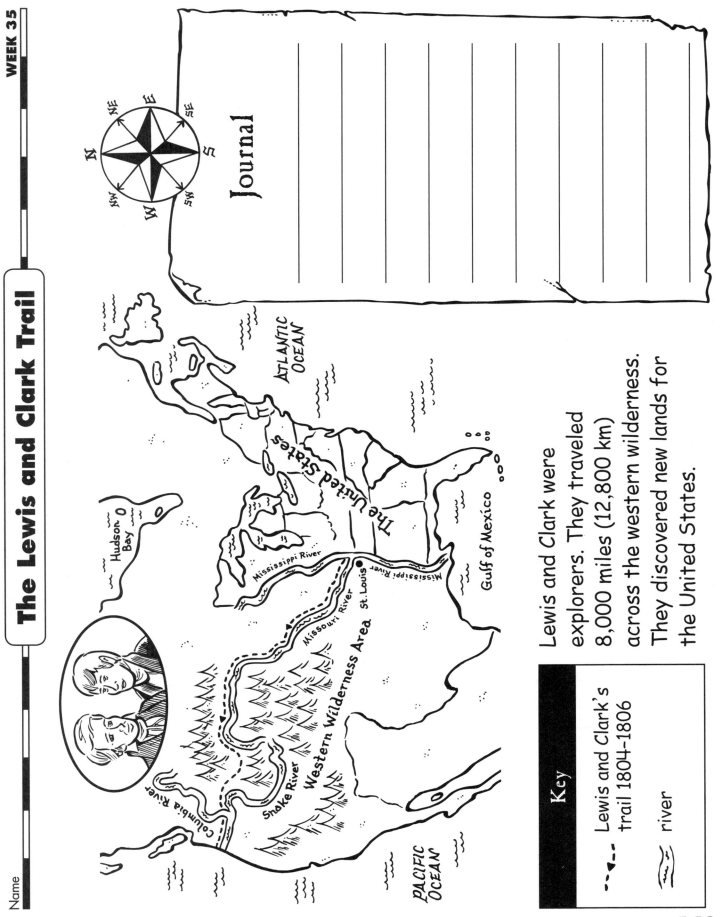

Journal

The United States

ATLANTIC OCEAN

Hudson Bay

Mississippi River

Missouri River

St. Louis

Mississippi River

Gulf of Mexico

Columbia River

Snake River

Western Wilderness Area

PACIFIC OCEAN

Lewis and Clark were explorers. They traveled 8,000 miles (12,800 km) across the western wilderness. They discovered new lands for the United States.

Key
- Lewis and Clark's trail 1804–1806
- river

The Lewis and Clark Trail

Monday

1. A person who travels to discover new things is called

   _____ .

2. Which two men explored the western wilderness?

   _____

Tuesday

1. The explorers started their journey in which city?

   _____

2. Lewis and Clark traveled to which ocean?

   _____

Wednesday

1. In 1804, was most of the United States settled or still wilderness?

   _____

2. Which river did Lewis and Clark follow most of the way?

   _____

The Lewis and Clark Trail

Thursday

1. How many miles did Lewis and Clark travel?

    _____

2. In what year did they start their journey? In what year did it end?

    _____

Friday

1. What did Lewis and Clark discover?

    _____

2. What happened to the western wilderness after 1806?

    _____

    _____

Challenge

Meriwether Lewis kept journals. He wrote about animals, plants, and people they saw along the trail. Pretend you were on the trail. On the map page, write a journal entry about what you saw.

A Neighborhood Plan

Introducing the Map

Ask students to name places in their neighborhood. They might name such places as a park, school, video store, or a fire station. Discuss how hard it would be to plan a neighborhood. Where would the community services be located? Would they build new businesses near homes or build a new soccer field? A city planner is the person who helps to make these decisions. City planners help city officials decide how to improve the community. City planners have a lot to think about.

Show students the map of a fictitious neighborhood. Talk about the different parts of the neighborhood. Read the labels and identify the different areas. Have students note the different homes, businesses, and community services in the neighborhood. Students should also notice the undeveloped land area. Tell students that they should be thinking about what to do with this area. They will be asked to come up with a plan on the challenge question.

Introducing Vocabulary

community services public places that provide for the needs of a community such as: schools, hospitals, police stations, and parks

neighborhood in a city, a small area where people live

vacant lot a piece of land that is empty

ANSWER KEY

Monday
1. a neighborhood
2. park; students may also say the schools because they have playgrounds as well.

Tuesday
1. east
2. west

Wednesday
1. a car wash
2. a school

Thursday
1. Yum Snacks
2. Maple Street, Third Street, and Fourth Street

Friday
1. school, library, city hall, and fire station—park is also a possibility
2. car wash, A-Z Stores, and video store

Challenge
Students should draw something in the empty lot that a community might need or want. Ideas might include such things as a grocery store, a police station, a recreation center, a mall, or a sports stadium.

First Street

A-Z STORES

FIRE STATION

Second Street

CAR WASH

CITY HALL

VIDEO STORE

Third Street

Elm Street

PARK

SCHOOL

YUM SNACKS

Maple Street

LIBRARY

Fourth Street

Draw what you would build in this vacant lot.

N W E S

The map shows a neighborhood. There is a vacant lot.
What would you build there? Make a plan.

Daily Geography

A Neighborhood Plan

WEEK 36

Monday

1. What does the map show?

   _____

2. Name a place where children can play.

   _____

Tuesday

1. Is City Hall east or west of the car wash?

   _____

2. Are the A-Z Stores east or west of the fire station?

   _____

Wednesday

1. What is north of the park?

   _____

2. What is east of the park?

   _____

A Neighborhood Plan

Thursday

1. Which business is northeast of the vacant lot?

   _____

2. The city park is located on which three streets?

   _____

   _____

Friday

1. Which community services are shown on this map?

   _____

   _____

2. Name the businesses on the map.

   _____

Challenge

Think about places that you would find in a neighborhood. Decide what you would put in the vacant lot. Draw a picture in the vacant lot and label it.

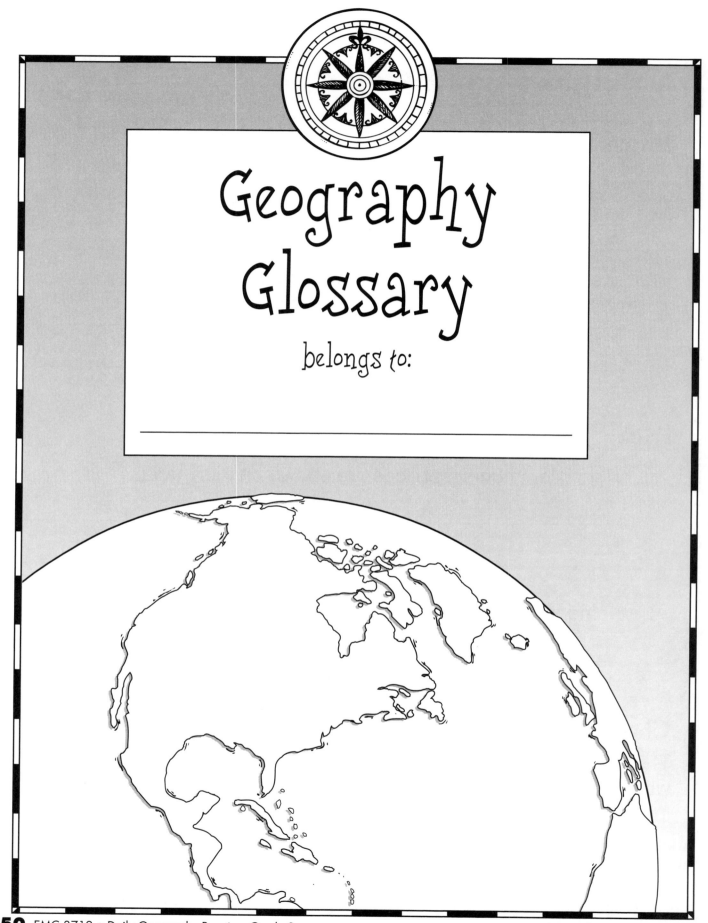

Geography Glossary

belongs to:

_____

address the house number, street, city, state, and zip code where a person usually receives mail

apartment a set of rooms to live in; usually one floor of a building

bay an area of ocean or lake partly surrounded by land; smaller than a gulf

bluegrass a grass that has tiny bluish-green buds

border a line on a map showing the edge of a city, state, or country

canyon a deep, narrow valley with steep sides

capital a city where the government of a country or state is located

cardinal directions north, south, east, and west (N, S, E, and W)

carnival a fair or festival with rides and games

city a very large or important town

coast land that is next to an ocean or sea

coastline the place where the land and the ocean meet; the outline of the coast

community a group of people who live together in the same area

community services public places that provide for the needs of a community such as: schools, hospitals, police stations, and parks

compass rose a symbol that shows directions on a map

continent one of the seven largest areas of land on Earth: Africa, Antarctica, Asia, Australia, Europe, North America, or South America

country a part of the world with its own borders and government; nation

county a part of a state; states are divided into counties

cultural landmark a place selected and pointed out as important to a group of people

culture a way of life, ideas, customs, and traditions

custom a way of acting; something that is done regularly

dairy farm a farm where cows are raised for their milk

degree a unit for measuring temperature (° is the symbol for degree)

desert dry, sandy land that gets little or no rain

duplex two houses that are attached by a wall

ecosystem a community of plants and animals

Ellipse an oval-shaped park in Washington, D.C.

equator an imaginary line that runs around the surface of the Earth

exhibit a public show

explore to travel in order to discover new things

fair a public show of farm products and animals, often with entertainment, games, and rides

ferry a boat used to carry people across water

forest a large area thickly covered with trees

fossil fuels natural gas, oil, and coal

glacier a large mass of ice

globe a round model of the Earth

Great Lakes five freshwater lakes: Superior, Michigan, Huron, Erie, and Ontario

grid a pattern of lines that form squares

gulf a large area of ocean partly surrounded by land; larger than a bay

harbor a sheltered body of water where ships anchor

highway a main road

history map a map that shows places or events from long ago

house a building where people live

human-made feature a part of Earth such as a city or a road created by people

index a list of place names and the grid squares where they are located

intermediate directions northeast, northwest, southeast, southwest (NE, NW, SE, SW)

intersection a place where two or more things meet and cross

island an area of land surrounded by water

lake a large body of fresh water surrounded by land

landform a natural feature on Earth's surface, like a mountain or hill

liberty freedom

livestock animals raised on a farm or ranch

location the site or position of something

map a drawing showing features of an area

map key a list that explains the symbols on a map

map scale a graphic that compares the distance on a map to the distance it represents

map sketch a rough drawing of a mental map

mental map a map that a person pictures in his or her mind

mineral something found in nature, like gold or silver

mining taking rocks and minerals out of the Earth

mobile home a large trailer that people live in

monument a building or statue that honors people or events

mountain a piece of land that has steep sides and a round or pointed peak; higher than a hill

mountain peak the highest point of a mountain

mountain range a group or chain of mountains

national forest a forest managed and protected by the government

natural resources materials supplied by nature such as forests, water, and minerals that are useful or necessary for life

neighborhood in a city, a small area where people live

North Pole the most northern point on Earth

ocean a large body of salt water

peninsula a piece of land that sticks out and is mostly surrounded by water

physical feature a natural part of Earth such as a mountain or an ocean

physical map a map that shows natural landforms and water

plains a large flat area of land

plateau high flat land; sometimes called a tableland

political map a map that shows human-made features

population the total number of people who live in a place

precipitation rain, snow, sleet, hail, or drizzle

product something that is made by a natural process, like corn, dairy cows, or minerals

product map a map that shows products such as corn, dairy cows, or minerals

region a large area with common features

river a large stream that flows into a larger river, lake, sea, or ocean

route a way to go from one place to another

sound a wide channel that connects two large bodies of water

South Pole the most southern point on Earth

state a group of people united under one government; a state can be a whole country, or part of a country, such as the United States

symbol a picture that stands for something real

temperature a measure of how hot or cold the air is

territory any large area of land

title the name of a map

tourist a person who travels on a vacation

tourist map a map that shows interesting places for people to see

town an area where people live and work; usually smaller than a city

trail a path

transportation how things or people are moved from place to place

vacant lot a piece of land that is empty

volcano an opening in the Earth's surface where lava, gases and ashes are forced out

waterfall a natural stream of water falling from a high place

waterway a river, ocean, or other body of water on which boats or ships travel

weather the condition of the air at a certain place and time

wilderness a natural place that is undisturbed by humans

My Glossary Words

As you work through the weekly maps, you may find other words that are new to you. Write the definitions of those words on this page.

_____

_____

_____

_____

_____

_____

_____

_____

_____

_____

_____

_____

_____

_____

_____

_____

_____

_____

_____

_____

_____